MW01515357

A FATHER'S SON

The Development of an Entrepreneur

The Business Life of Randy Boyd
Through a Father's Perspective

BY TOM BOYD

A Father's Son
The Development of an Entrepreneur

by Tom Boyd

Copyright © 2018 by Tom Boyd

ISBN 978-0-9905081-4-4

Printed in the United States

305 PORTSMOUTH RD
KNOXVILLE TN 37909
VISIONRUN.COM

EXCEPTIONALISM

It is obvious, of course, that I am proud of my son. His deeds and actions along with the following testimonials support my beliefs. – T.B.

I do believe that our leaders should exemplify "American Exceptionalism." Our leaders should be creative, innovative, and problem solvers. These people need not be career politicians bent on compromise and maintaining power, but instead, career "doers," versatile people who have ideas and courage to stand by them to fruition. From what I have seen and heard, you are the person I would like to see represent this model of American (and Tennessean) Exceptionalism as our governor.

— David Needs, Professor History and Leadership
Carson-Newman University,
sharing his thoughts on meeting Randy
in Hamblen County, April 2017

My biggest draw towards Randy is the fact that he came from "Anywhere, TN" The New Hopewell community and all the little communities in South Knoxville are much like every little town in Tennessee. They are close-knit people who care about their neighbors and their communities. I think Randy epitomizes these traits.

Randy is proof that if you are determined, set goals, and work hard, anyone can accomplish anything. More importantly, after accomplishing goals, he sets new goals to continue moving forward, helping others to reach their goals. If we could all be as dedicated to reaching our goals and helping others as he is, how much better would our communities, state, and nation be?

I spend time at New Hopewell, South Doyle High, and all over South Knoxville, so I see the streets he traveled and the halls he walked, but the "path" he followed is the "road less taken." I'm willing to follow him down this road and hope that Tennessee is as well.

— John Staser
New Hopewell Elementary Resource Officer

Randy chaired the 2014 United Way of East Tennessee Campaign – shattering all previous campaign records.

Randy Boyd is called. I'm pretty certain he's called to give back. His head, his heart, and his soul are in the right place. He really, truly cares about people. I've seen it in his eyes. I've seen him work and meet people who have had very difficult challenges in their life, and he was moved to do something about it. He doesn't want a lot of fanfare. He doesn't want a lot of attention. He has a heart and soul for people.

— Ben Landers, CEO
United Way of Knoxville Interview October 2016

I did not know that Randy was a first-generation college graduate. It is pretty awesome to see that he is a self-made individual who maybe didn't have the opportunities that some people do and created those along the way for himself. He is now paying it back to others in the community to give them every opportunity to be successful in life, which is pretty remarkable.

— Doug Kose, CEO
Big Brothers Big Sisters

When you meet Randy Boyd, you can tell this man is committed to his principles, he's committed to all the people he interacts with, he's committed to his vision. It is easy to tell that he wants the best for people; he wants the best for his company, for his employees, for the young people that he serves. I know that many of the organizations that he's involved with focus on youth and youth development. I think he's committed to helping as many young people as possible have bright, strong futures. I think Randy's committed.

— Chip Reed, President
Junior Achievement East Tennessee

Well, he's been invaluable to Knoxville and our community and all of East Tennessee; really, I would say from education's perspective, he has transformed it, certainly here in Tennessee. It's rare that someone, an individual comes along who is really that transformational. He is one of those rare human beings who really has made a significant difference in our educational system.

— Susan Richardson Williams, President
SRW Associates, former TN Republican Party Chairman

When I think about Randy Boyd, I think about the scout laws, the scout oath, and when you a talk about the 12 points of the scout law, it's just who Randy is.

— David Williams, Scout Executive
Great Smoky Mountain Council, Boy Scouts of America

Randy's a sleep-on-the-ground scoutmaster, and what that means is there are a lot of people involved in scouting, and they come to all the meetings, they participate and they do a great job for us, but some of the guys, some of the dads or scoutmasters actually go out into the wilderness and participate in all the hikes and camp-outs. If you are a certain age, you don't really want to sleep on the ground, but Randy's definitely a sleep-on-the-ground kind of leader, and he pulled me into that, and we had some terrific nights with the kids on the wilderness trails.

— Tracy Thompson, CEO
Peoples Bank

Yeah, Randy's had all the big jobs in the scout council. He's been in charge of the friends of scouting campaign. He's been the council president. He was the vice chairman of our capital fundraising campaign and raised a bunch of money for our scout camp down on Watts Bar Lake. He's done all those things, but Randy's what we call a muddy-boots or a sleep-on-the-

ground Boy Scout leader. We have great volunteers to do those big jobs, but some of them don't even own a scout uniform, but Randy did the big jobs, and he also did the little jobs with the boys – 10 years as a pack master and seven years as a boy scout leader.

— Logan Hickman

AWARDS AND HONORS

Pinnacle Entrepreneur of the Year (1998)

Tennessee Business CEO of the Year (2008)

Ernst and Young Entrepreneur of the Year
in the Southeast U.S. (2009)

Inducted into the Junior Achievement
of East Tennessee Hall of Fame (2009)

University of Tennessee College of Business
Entrepreneur of the Year (2012)

National College Access Network Person of the Year (2013)

East Tennessee Community Design Center,
Bruce McCarty Community Impact Award (2013)

Tennessee Business Roundtable Gordon Fee
Impact of the Year Award (2014)

Pinnacle James Haslam Impact of the Year (2014)

University of Tennessee Alumni of the Year Award (2014)

SCHAD Knoxville Person of the Year Award (2015)

American Red Cross of Chattanooga
Humanitarian of the Year (2016)

Boy Scouts of America Great Smoky Mountain
Council Distinguished Citizen of the Year (2017)

Boys and Girls Club Gift of Hope Award (2017)

Tennessee Geographic Alliance Visionary of the Year (2017)

DEDICATION

This book is dedicated to my wife, Sandi Burdick. I want to thank her for her patience and love. She's my best friend and confidante. She has been more than understanding while I have devoted so much of my time to business endeavors.

TOM BOYD

FOREWORD

This book is an attempt to provide a view of my son's successes as an entrepreneur through my eyes. I hope he will agree with most of it, but if he doesn't, remember the father is always right.

When I previously decided to write a book for my children, which was about my "early years" growing up in the rural South, I was attempting to give them an understanding of events and the influences they had on me. In a small way, I wanted to show them that life now is no different from then — it just has different players. These early years made a lasting impression on me and effected many of my future business decisions, and in turn influenced some of my son's.

As I had just miraculously reached my 80th birthday, I realized life was indeed passing. There were a lot of things I wanted to reconstruct in my memory of my son. I only knew my side of the story, and I hoped that by writing the book, I could blend his thoughts with mine, creating a full picture of my relationship with him and how, over the years, our lives in business took similar paths.

Randal (Randy) Deward Boyd was born on October 24, 1959. Starting from when he was ten years old, he enthusiastically embraced and has perpetuated the life of entrepreneurship. Throughout his life, he has demonstrated exemplary leadership as an innovative businessman, dedicated son, husband and father, a selfless philanthropist, and a never-wavering commitment to public service.

Randy, being Randy, over the years has kept a written track of his adventures, successes, and failures. He never had any intention of anyone else ever reading them, but I convinced him that it was for me, and he gave me permission to use excerpts from them in this book.

At certain points within, I will insert some of Randy's stories. I believe the reader will find that he is an extraordinary man and son who has worked all his life to be the best he can be, while at the same time following his motto:

Service is the rent we pay for the space we occupy.

— Harry D. Strunk

CONTENTS

SECTION I

THE PATH TO FATHERHOOD

The path to fatherhood . . . sounds like I had a plan. Nothing could have been farther from the truth. While I have always believed that opportunity is the product of perspiration, the fact is that destiny and fate are always working in our lives.

My early years were spent working to get out of the cotton fields. I dreamed of traveling the world and making my mark in business. It's a little embarrassing to say that marriage and fatherhood really did not cross my mind. Then, in stepped destiny and fate.

The following pages detail Randy's mom and our lives before Randy, Randy's formative years, his introduction to business and entrepreneurship, and business lessons learned the hard way.

Time and events: Without having a reference to time and events at certain junctures of this story, it would be impossible for the reader to relate to this era without a comparison to the present one.

As this is about being an entrepreneur, amounts of money are quite often mentioned. Without a comparison of the value of money today, the sums quoted would be misleading. The 2018 dollar equivalent to figures in this book will be listed in parentheses after each dollar amount. One also needs to be able to associate with the events of the time, so they can walk along side the participants at certain periods in this book.

CHAPTER 1

BEFORE THERE WAS A RANDY

The year was 1957. Eisenhower had been elected president by a landslide in the fall of 1956. Richard Nixon was his vice president.

Russia started the space race with the launch of *Sputnik 1*. The Viet Cong guerrillas attacked South Vietnam, the first peacetime nuclear reactor plant opened in Pennsylvania, and Elvis Presley bought Graceland.

The inflation rate was 3.34%, the average house cost $12,220, the average monthly rent was $90.00, and the average yearly wage was $4,550 or $2 per hour.

You could get a dozen eggs for 28 cents and a gallon of gas for 24 cents. You could spend $1 to buy things that would now cost you $10 in 2018.

Sadly, the final episode of the *I Love Lucy* show aired.

Every child must start somewhere, but before Randy could come along, I had to find my way to Germany to meet his mother.

I joined the Army in 1957, which was not planned. I had just attended one quarter of college and had decided I didn't want to wait four years to see the world and experience a few adventures. I had just finished a book on William Walker, a gentleman who went to Central America in 1856 and started a revolution that made him the president of Nicaragua.

I thought if he could do that, so could I. Of course I had no idea how, but decided to head that way and try my luck. At the time I was 19 years old.

To start this adventure, I packed my bags and left Chicago, where I had been working at the time. I had $50 dollars in my pocket. Looking at the map, I decided that hitchhiking out of Chicago would be difficult, so I bought a ticket on the Greyhound bus to St. Louis, Missouri. From that starting point, I began hitchhiking to Los Angeles, which would get me closer to Central America. I planned on stopping there for a while and earning enough money to get me south.

The trip across the United States took me down Route 66 all the way into Los Angeles. I wouldn't take anything for this adventure. I hitchhiked during the day and slept under bridges at night. Along the way I met many interesting people who were making the same trip, but for different reasons.

Sometime later, Route 66 became the basis of a television series. The towns I passed through no long exist with the same vibrancy they did then. While interstates are great, they basically wiped out most of the Route 66 towns.

I arrived in Los Angeles seven days after I started and had $20 dollars left. I rented a room on Maple Street, which was just off the central square in downtown Los Angeles. In those days, this central square was a sleepy little area with very few people. Now it is the center of L.A.

I assumed finding a job would be as easy as it had been in Chicago. Unfortunately, I didn't understand the dynamics of L.A. at the time. There were very few factory jobs, and the pioneering, high-tech types of industry that we know today had already begun. When I finally found work after three days of searching, I was down to my last $2. I wasn't really worried as I thought I could go three or four days without eating if necessary. I was expecting to start work on a Tuesday and get paid on Friday. The first day, they told me that they always held back one week's pay. I knew I couldn't possibly last that long without food.

While searching for work, I would pass the recruiting offices of the Army, Air Force, and Navy each day as they were located on the square where I was staying. I guess from day one I had contemplated using this as my back-up plan if my venture to Central America didn't pan out.

By this time, it had been a couple of days since I had any food, so that made the decision easy. There wasn't any alternative to joining one of the branches of the military. I first applied at the Navy recruitment office as they had great billboards touting world travel. This sounded great, but when they told me I had to enlist for four years, I didn't think I was that hungry yet. The same four-year enlistment was required for the Air Force. By the time I reached the Army recruiting office, my decision was basically made for me as I had run out of options.

I will never forget entering the Army recruiting office and saying to the person I saw, "If you can guarantee me food today, I'm yours." He said, "the minute you sign, we give you *a flying ten*." I said, "I'm your man." I was then told that as I was volunteering, I could ask to be assigned to the kind of work I wanted to do. An hour before, I was not considering joining anything. I looked around the recruitment office and saw a stand with a sign on it of an MP (military policeman). I said, "I'll take that."

This decision took me on a circuitous route that led to meeting Randy's mother.

I took the ten dollars and went directly out and ate so much I nearly got sick. After taking care of my hunger, I began second-guessing myself. Being naïve about these things, I thought maybe I could go back to their office and tell them I had changed my mind. Knowing young farm-boy recruits, they were aware of this. The minute I came back in the office, they immediately gave me a physical exam, and a sergeant took us to a waiting bus. Before I knew it, I was in Fort Ord, California. We were quickly moved to a barrack in the middle of the fort area. All this time someone was bellowing and giving orders that kept us constantly moving until bedtime.

A couple of guys I met on the train from Los Angeles to Fort Ord had an idea. They also had not yet accepted that they were in the Army. Around midnight, they decided this experience was not for them, so they climbed out the barrack's window with every intention to depart the Army. This second-thought thinking must have been common during the first day or so, which is the reason the barracks were located in the Fort's center. Every building looked the same, and they didn't know where to go. It made no difference because within the first 20 minutes, the MPs picked them up and returned them to our barracks. Their first day in the Army was spent cleaning a coal stove in the mess hall. There were a lot of other guys cleaning it too.

The following day, the Army really, really set in for all of us. They shaved our heads and gave us so many shots that we simply fell into line.

I was then moved to Fort Lewis, Washington for basic training and then to Fort Gordon outside of Augusta, Georgia for MP training. This was in September and October of 1957, and there could not have been a hotter place on earth. After eight weeks of training, we were shipped to Fort Dix, New Jersey for processing to our next assignment.

My next lesson in how the Army operated took place at Fort Dix. The Army is big on paperwork and tests, regardless of the person. On my first day there, a sergeant came in and told me that I had my choice of where I could be stationed in Europe. This is basically unheard of in the Army. The sergeant told me that my GT (General Technical) score was very high and that qualified me to select the place I wanted to serve.

Actually, I didn't know how to do anything mechanical or practical, but all the reading I had done made their tests very easy. Since GT scores always follow you through your Army life, they gave me the opportunity to experience some interesting jobs.

Once again, chance is what life is all about. I was given the choice of working at the United States Embassy in Paris, France or the European Headquarters in Heidelberg, Germany. I had decided on Paris, which would have eliminated the opportunity to meet my future wife, but a soldier who had been in both places sold me on Heidelberg as that was the seat of Army Command plus a beautiful city.

My choosing Heidelberg set in motion my meeting Randy's mom.

At approximately the same time, Randy's mother, Delores "Dale" Rector, started her adventure from the other side of the country, where she lived with her parents in Knoxville, Tennessee. When she told her parents that she was going to join the Women's Army Corp, they went ballistic, but Dale, showing the same determination that her future son would, won the battle of wills.

She boarded a bus for training at Fort McClellan, Alabama. She then went to Fort Benjamin Harris in Indianapolis for administrative training and then on to Fort McPherson, Georgia for a short time. She was eventually assigned to Heidelberg, Germany to the same command where I was assigned.

She was assigned to a general and worked on a top-secret project called "Seventh Heaven." She had the opportunity to fly around Germany in the general's helicopter and developed a lifelong love of flying. She had a top-secret clearance for this job, and I must admit, she kept to her directive not to share information. It was only when I began writing this book that I really became aware of what she was doing when I met her. She would simply say, "I'm a secretary." I was assigned to the European HQ at the time, and I had heard of this project but never knew what it involved. Recently when I asked her about it, she would still not say what they were doing. I also had a top-secret clearance, but the only secrets I had to keep were where the best doughnuts could be found and when they were hot. This is not quite true – with my clearance I was involved in projects that would protect the West from Russia. How we would do that, if disclosed, would still create an international uproar with Germany and France today.

When Dale's program was completed, she was transferred to Kaiserslautern, Germany, where she finished her army career with the Army newspaper *Stars and Stripes*.

We met in the spring of 1958 and were married in Basel, Switzerland on September 12, 1958. It was the year the movie *The Bridge on the River Kwai* was showing, and our commanding officer felt it was such a good military movie that he required all the soldiers in his command to attend. We had the typical club for soldiers. While this movie was showing, they had a drawing at the club, and Dale and I both won a ticket to the movie. Our first date. Who doesn't believe in destiny?

She always had more pull than I did, but I enjoyed the company I was stationed with and the duties I had, but one day she told me that she was being transferred to Kaiserslautern. The next day my commanding officer came in and threw my transfer papers at me, very angry that I hadn't requested a transfer through proper channels. I didn't know what he was talking about but realized Dale had been instrumental in my reassignment. I was reassigned to the provost marshall's office in Kaiserslautern, which wasn't a bad gig.

I have strong opinions about who should be an entrepreneur. I'm not really sure you can train a person to be one. When I was stationed in Germany, I always had a desire to make extra money on my own. At that time the Army paid privates $97 per month.

Although we call ourselves entrepreneurs now, I don't believe I had ever heard that word until I was in my 60s. When I attempted my first business, I didn't perceive myself as anything but a guy wanting to make an extra buck. I spent most of my life being called a businessman. I'm not sure what happened to that classification or when the term entrepreneur became commonplace. The original word for an "entrepreneur" was "undertaker", or someone who does things well. I didn't really want to be an undertaker, but I loved the idea of being an entrepreneur.

My options as a new entrepreneur were limited, but I quickly took advantage of all of them and created a few new ones on my own.

The Army had rules that all soldiers were allowed to have coupons for x number of packs of cigarettes each month plus gas and alcohol. Obviously all soldiers didn't smoke, most didn't own cars, and a few didn't drink. I worked some with a German civilian, and he was always asking to buy my coupons. Once he told me what he would pay, a light was turned on. I eventually had over 50 soldiers selling me their coupons, and by the end of 1958, I was making over $500 per month – compare that to the average U.S. income of $4,550 a year!

I quickly realized that the coupon purchasing couldn't grow past my company friends, so I was continuously looking for something new to sell my German contacts. The Germans were short on everything, but our government was wise to the specific products they wanted to restrict from the German people. Coffee was in high demand, but our PX system had a very limited quota on these and other products that they deemed essential.

My goal was to find something that the Germans wanted, but didn't know they did, and where the PX had no quota.

I tried many things that failed, but one day I was eating a bag of barbecue potato chips, and the thought struck me that I had never seen any of these in a German store. I bought some bags and took them to the local store that I visited and offered some to the owner. He loved them. I suggested we put some samples on his counter and see if people would buy them. They did. At one time, when purchasing a cartload at the PX, the manager said, "I can't keep these in stock. Do you know that our PX is the world's largest purchaser of barbecue potato chips?"

I don't know what the lesson here is, but I do know that I learned that if one is creative, there's always a pony to ride and that I would forever be an entrepreneur.

During our European stint, I won a car in a poker game. It wasn't much, and I knew nothing about cars and neither did Dale. All we knew was that it would run, but we didn't know how far, so we decided that we would take a trip to France and Italy, and if the car quit on us, we would just leave it. We financed our trip by trading government-issued gas and cigarette coupons along the way. Later we calculated back from Randy's birth date and determined that he was conceived in Rome, Italy in January of 1959. While Dale was pregnant with Randy, we traveled to Holland and Spain. We also visited the World's Fair in Brussels in 1958.

I firmly believe that kids start learning when they are conceived, and a lot of their lives are built around this unknown time. Randy has always been excited about traveling and learning about other countries. As of this writing, he has visited over 72 countries. As a side note, both his mother and I love German bratwurst. When Randy and I travel anywhere in Germany, we are both looking for bratwurst. We can never find the kind I brag about, but everything tasted differently at age19.

During Dale's pregnancy, we were reassigned to Frankfort, Germany, and Dale worked only a short time. We lived on the German economy until she was required to fly home. The Army had restrictions on how late in pregnancy one could fly. Dale left Germany in August of 1959, and Randy was born on October 24, 1959. Dale and I were both only 21 years old. Looking back, when you are that young, you basically grow up with your children.

Before she left Germany, we chose his name. Not a simple thing to do. I wanted him to have the name that would fit a president, and she wanted him to be a writer. I got the "Randal" part, and she got the "Deward" part, so that is how he is stuck with his name. Eventually we compromised, and "Randy" was the name we agreed to use.

I heard about my son's birth through a Telex message. Phone calls were too expensive then, and of course, we didn't have email. A German gentleman, Rudy Snell, brought the story of his arrival. They knew I had been waiting for it, but after Rudy picked it up, he held it until they got me out of the office, so the first celebration for Randy was by Germans. Randy later married a girl whose mother was German.

Can you imagine having your first son and knowing you will not see him for months? I really think the waiting was a great experience for forming the expectations to seeing him for the first time. I arrived in Knoxville in April of 1960, and our story begins.

CHAPTER 2

NEW KID ON THE BLOCK/ FORMATIVE YEARS

When Dale and I got out of the Army, we returned to Dale's home in Knoxville. Unfortunately there weren't any jobs available in that area. Within a month Dale and I moved to Chicago. Randy would spend his first year as a Chicago baby.

As I have said earlier, what one is exposed to before birth and experiences during the first few years seem to follow a person all their life. This has certainly been true for Randy.

We lived in an apartment that was about three blocks from the Chicago Cubs baseball stadium. While we never went to a game, from our window we could always hear the roar of the crowds on game days. I was never a baseball fan, so Randy couldn't have gotten his love of baseball from me. He has always been a fanatical fan of baseball, so much so, that in later life he bought a minor league team that was affiliated with the Cubs. As an enthusiastic fan, he makes as many Cubs games as possible, and when the major league Cubs won the World Series in 2016, they awarded Randy and his wife, Jenny, a championship ring.

In 1961, Dale was pregnant with our first daughter, so she and Randy moved back to her parents' home in Knoxville to have our child. Gigi Michelle was born on December 31, 1961.

As we rejoiced, we quickly realized there were major complications with her health that required the care of more than one person. We sold our catering business in Chicago, and I moved to Knoxville. As luck would have it, I was able to obtain a job as a traveling salesman, and the company allowed me to be based out of Knoxville.

We bought a house on Clinton Highway in Knoxville, and the four of us moved into our first home. Unfortunately my job required extensive travel. Since our daughter required round-the-clock attention, and as I was away most of the time, we sold our home to move back to Dale's parents' home, so her mother could help in taking care of Gigi.

Our daughter died after only 18 months. She was a beautiful child, and her loss devastated us. Randy was only four at the time, but he played with her constantly – one of her joys I'm sure she took with her.

My new job required that I work eight southern states, from Mississippi to Northern Virginia. When I accepted the job, the owner offered me a fair salary, but I declined and told him that I believed that I would work harder than anyone else and wanted to work on a commission basis only. He advised me against it. He said, "You may not be getting a paycheck, and you have a family to think about." Within the first year, I made four times what he had offered.

When I moved later into my own company, I always remembered that when people get rewarded for their efforts, they will always produce more.

At the beginning of my first company, I started off with the general practice of having an assembly line that worked at a prearranged rate. At this time, this was considered the best way to have a steady rate of production. We had five assembly lines with 20 people on each. I worked each of these lines with them to learn how they felt and also what they were capable of doing. I found that I could do twice what any of them was doing, but then, I had the motivation of rewarding myself for what I did.

I truly believe that anyone can do anything; sometimes they just have to have an opportunity. Knowing they could do better and at the same time reap the rewards, I took the dramatic step of destroying one assembly line over a weekend. When they came to work on Monday, I asked each of them to go to a particular station that was assigned to them only. At each of these stations, they had the tools to do 20 different parts of making a complete product.

The first reaction was consternation. You could see fright in their eyes. When I explained to them the possible benefits if they could do it, some accepted; most didn't.

Each was to build an electric energizer (an electric box that was used to electrify wire fences, to contain cattle) from the ground up. This required soldering, inserting circuit boards, testing, and labeling. I explained that I had faith in them, and if they would try this, I would guarantee them that the quota would not go up, and they would be rewarded for their effort. The argument that really closed them was that as we were open 24 hours a day and seven days a week, I didn't care when they worked. They could work ten hours a day and take three off and work any hours of the day. This gave them the opportunity to pick their hours, and be with their kids when they needed to be. In other words, they were each their own boss. It made them entrepreneurs, rather than just laborers.

Within the first week, one lady stood up and said, "I'm done for the day." She had been working four hours. Within a month everyone on the line was beating the quota.

When someone builds a product by themselves, they take ownership. Part of the requirements were that each unit they built had to go through an inspection. This product, if not built right, could be lethal, so 100% inspection was required. Products on the assembly line had a normal defective rate of 7% and would have to be reworked. These women brought that rate down to less than .5% percent.

As they were proud of the product that was built by them, they requested to have labels with their name on it so that they could affix it to the unit showing it was their product.

These women went on to work for me over 20 years.

This is a father/son book, and the purpose is to show how this work environment influenced some of Randy's later thoughts.

The following is an excerpt from Randy's later writings:

"I have realized that it's only when people are instructed to blindly obey directives from someone not directly involved that the processes get complicated, usually inefficient, and most importantly, frustrating and demoralizing for those doing it. Today, my operating philosophy continues to be to give responsibility and key decision-making to the front lines as much as possible."

As a traveling salesman, if you don't make a sale, you don't eat. My average week consisted of over 2,000 miles of driving. Most weeks I left early Monday morning and didn't return home until late on Friday night. At least once a month, I would be such a distance from home that I would spend the weekend out. Consequently, for the first eight years of Randy's life, I was home less than 80 days a year.

This left the early training of Randy's formative years up to his mother. She did an excellent job as she did with all our children. Dale's expectations for our children were very high. As a result, from their very early ages, she did many things to train and educate them.

Nightly family dinners were always special as Dale would teach the kids proper eating etiquette and always prepared meals that represented different countries. She posted words they had to learn to spell on the refrigerator door, and each day she would quiz them. She read them books that were over their heads, but this was her way of teaching them to strive for higher expectations of themselves.

One of the first things she did after Randy was born was to buy a set of encyclopedias. Over the years, I believe she must have read or made the kids read every one of them – from A to Z.

Randy's sister, Autumn Rene, was born on July 5, 1964, and his youngest sister, Stephanie Mia, on December 5, 1967. Randy has always been the big brother and still is. I'm proud to say that my kids take care of each other and are the best of friends.

Much the way Dale began early education at home, I began Randy's introduction to the family business world as well.

The summer Randy was seven, I took him on a sales trip with me for two weeks. We traveled through Virginia and North and South Carolina. I had an expense allowance of $12 dollars per day for meals and lodging. Obviously we didn't travel first class, but to a seven-year-old it wasn't important. What is important is what he learned from that trip and put into practice in his later business life. We stayed in boarding houses that charged $2 a night with breakfast included.

As we made our sales calls on hardware and feed and seed stores, Randy was a great asset as the buyers loved him. When we stopped at feed stores, Randy would instantly start climbing on the feed sacks. These things can be quite dirty, and by the end of the day you could hardly see his face. Years later when he had his own distributing company, he called on these same stores. One day, one of the buyers asked us if we would play golf with him after work. The golfer we teamed up with had his right arm missing (he had lost it in the Korean War). I didn't know what to expect, and Randy said he didn't believe the guy could hit the ball. He did and he beat us.

That night I said, "Randy, if a one-arm man can do that, you can do anything." He's followed that thought all his life.

Outward Bound—
Three Oak Ridgers and two Knoxvillians departed July 20 for Children's International Village being held at the foot of Mt. Fuji near Gotemba, Japan, in a YMCA camp. The village is being attended for a month by four 11-year-old delegates and an adult chaperone from each of ten countries. On the way back to Tennessee the group will tour Tokyo and spend four days in Honolulu, arriving Aug. 24. From left are, Danny Russell, Oak Ridge, Randy Boyd, Knoxville, Ann Waters, Becky Halperin, Oak Ridge, and Cam McCoin, Knoxville.

Randy's formative years weren't all about learning the business. When he was 11 he had the opportunity to travel to Japan with a program called "Children's International Summer Village." This gave him a chance to interact with children his age from all over the world. I know that for many years later, he corresponded with a lot of the friends he made through this experience. Meeting other people of different races gives one a better understanding that all people are created equal, and the color of one's skin, race, or religion does not separate them from each other.

I have never known Randy to say a derogatory word about another person and am absolutely certain that he does not know the word "prejudice." I believe this early interaction was partly responsible.

I never listened to music, so I was surprised when Randy became such a big fan of the Beatles. Later in life, he went to London, England and met with the Beatles' manager.

While there, Randy acquired a signed page of music written by the Beatles. Randy's interest in music has continued; today his wife, Jenny, owns a music venue.

Randy loved his time in the Boy Scouts. Even today, he frequently quotes the Boy Scout's motto: *Be prepared.* I believe this motto has had a lot of meaning to him as I have never known him to go into a meeting, activity, or any other venture without thoroughly preparing himself. He is always truly prepared. He has spent his life following the Boy Scout Law: *Be Trustworthy, Loyal, Helpful, Friendly, Courteous, Kind, Obedient, Cheerful, Thrifty, Brave, Clean, and Reverent.* Most importantly, I have never known him to tell a lie.

CHAPTER 3

INTRODUCTION TO BUSINESS

In 1968, I started Fi-Shock, Inc. The company was created to manufacture a device to prevent dogs from overturning garbage cans. It was designed to transmit an electric shock to the dogs when they touched the cans. At the time I obtained my patent, nearly all garbage cans were metal, and my device worked great on them.

One month after I started the business, Rubbermaid came out with plastic cans and virtually wiped out the use of metal cans. My great idea and product were instantly obsolete. The best laid plans!

We had just set up a four-person assembly line to manufacture the garbage can device. The garbage can device emitted 500 volts of electricity, which was enough to deter dogs but not enough to contain a larger animal. As this was the only product that we had, and I knew that it was a vanishing market, we were desperate to do something.

Randy went to work with me most days when he wasn't in school. He was there the day that we found that we could add an additional capacitor to the transformer and add another 500 volts, an amount that could effectively keep a horse or cow contained.

Randy stuck a volt meter to this new device, and it showed 1000 volts. Randy was so excited about this that I gave him credit for creating a new product. This product became the lynch pin in our company. We were now in the cattle containment business. This product disrupted the industry and quickly captured a huge market share. Over the next several years we sold over three million of them. We went on to manufacture over 800 products, but this was the forerunner of them all. I think this was one of his best lessons – that you try and try again until you find something that works. Any business is a gamble, but you never lose if you never quit.

Randy quickly learned that developing products that disrupt an industry are a true path to success. When Randy was 16 years old, I found a company in Chattanooga that manufactured buttons. They had millions to pack in bags of ten and 20. It was a hand-operated deal, and I thought it would be a great training tool for him to learn how businesses operated and make money. He had to do his own billing, collect the money, and hire people to do it.

At first, he hired a few of his friends that went to school with him, and he set up some tables in our garage. He applied some of the lessons he learned earlier working in my company – you reward people for what they do, not for a position. He paid the boys a set price per bag so that they could earn as much as they were capable of or wanted to earn.

Randy had worked on the assembly line and was observant. He came to me one day and asked if I knew someone who could automate his process and cut out part of the labor. As it happened, I had a brilliant guy that did motion study for me and who was also a designer of automated equipment. He made Randy an automatic conveyor belt with a machine that sealed the bags all in one motion. His profits tripled.

The bags of buttons were being used by the button manufacturer for a contract they had with the Saudi Arabian Army. Their soldiers were issued field jackets with two extra packs with each jacket. Unfortunately, there just weren't that many soldiers, so the contract wasn't renewed. It's probably a good thing as I wouldn't have wanted him to be known as the "Button King."

Randy's introduction to my company was a perfect learning time for him. When I started Fi-Shock, I had only owned and operated one other business. When I was 22, my wife and I were living in Chicago, and I was working part-time at my uncle's restaurant. I noticed that most of the catering trucks serving food around Chicago were really old. When I was in Los Angeles before I joined the Army, I had seen these really neat, stainless-steel catering trucks and thought these would go over well in the Chicago area. I had no idea what I was doing but knew I didn't want to work for someone else. I took the plunge and borrowed $5,000 from my uncle to buy one of these trucks.

The year was 1961. Costs of everything had gone up substantially in the past four years, and the world seemed to be moving faster.

We had a new president, John F. Kennedy, Yuri Gagarin was the first human in space, the Peace Corp was established, and the Berlin Wall was started. We mounted the first attempt to overthrow Castro with the invasion called "Bay of Pigs." Everyone was afraid of a nuclear attack from Russia. Naively, we were taught in school to get under our desks in case of an attack.

Buying an average home still cost $12,500, only a slight increase over 1957, average income rose to $5,315, a dozen eggs jumped to 30 cents, and gas remained at 27 cents per gallon.

The value of $1.00 then is worth $8.57 in 2018. Inflation was down to 1%.

Some of my favorite new shows aired, the "West Side Story," "Breakfast at Tiffany's," "The Hustler" and the "The Guns of Navarone."

There were numerous new TV series – "Wagon Train," "Bonanza," "Gunsmoke," "Andy Griffin," and "Perry Mason." Alfred Hitchcock started his long run of TV hits with "Alfred Hitchcock Presents."

While I had never been in business before, I did know that when you start your first business, you are forced to learn quickly or lose. I'm not totally sure what I learned, but one thing I am certain of – if a new entrepreneur follows all the rules, they will most likely get discouraged and quit. I had no idea about licenses, taxes, having a corporate charter, or cash flow.

I do not remember starting this business with anything but a license plate for the truck and a license for the right to sell. There were no lawyers involved, and I followed no regulations. The first lesson the catering truck business taught me was you have to earn more than you spend. To support the business, I also purchased a restaurant that I used to prepare the food for the catering truck, and it was also open to the public. The restaurant added to my knowledge of business and regulations and gave me the opportunity to work with an accountant who taught me the basics of business finance. To the best of my recollection, I had the first such catering truck east of the Mississippi River. Now they are everywhere.

So when I started Fi-Shock at age 29, I wasn't going in completely blind. I had worked for a company selling electric fences across the southern United States and knew my new product, its potential, and the marketplace. I recognized that the industry needed a type of electric charger that was inexpensive and effective. My first product was an energizer for dog containment but quickly moved up to a full line of products and accessories. Once Fi-Shock was started, Randy was old enough to frequently go to work with me and that gave him the opportunity to pick up a wide variety of business skills in his early years.

If one really knew when they started a business about all the problems they would experience, they probably would not do it. Problems and road blocks certainly can't be anticipated, and if one wants to grow, constantly trying new ideas is a must. If you invent new things, that is exactly what they are; however, there are no guidelines to guarantee these new inventions will be a success.

Fi-Shock's first product did not work well enough to create a market for a viable business. As I mentioned earlier, our addition of a simple capacitor gave us our first profitable product. Randy experienced all these failures with me, but also the successes. I think when he started his business, he thought that with all his experiences with me, that now he knew how to produce a product without failures. Life and business don't work that way. Instead, he struggled with his new product.

My experience is that there is a 90% chance you can't get a new product right the first time. I do think he gained strength in knowing that his father had experienced his own share of failures and took motivation from the fact that I never quit and succeeded in at least half of them.

One specific example was our entry into the electronic bug killer business. We had reached the point with our existing product line that we simply couldn't see a large market even if we captured a lion's share of the world market. The bug killer product concept was already on the market, but we felt the leading company wasn't marketing it correctly.

Our first mistake was to copy our competitor's product as there were not any patents on them. We developed an identical product with a different cosmetic housing, which worked great in the lab. We got electrical approvals from Canada with the CE certification and in the U.S. with the UL certification. (UL means a product meets the quality and safety standards of Underwriters Laboratories. CE is a similar approval signifying it meets European standards, and is more commonly used in Canada than UL.) We were selected as having the top-rated product by *Consumer Reports*. With this assurance, one would think we had a winner, and we did. Within months we had doubled the company sales and had orders that would have doubled business again within three months.

Then our service department called me requesting an urgent meeting. Our top-rated product with all the testing that was done was flawed because of the type of plastic polyethylene that we used to separate the wires on the killing grid. We had determined that if a wire was placed 3/8 of an inch from another, one wire would be the ground and the other the live wire. The distance was determined by how far a certain voltage would jump to electrocute the bugs flying through the killing grids. The inside of a bug killer had a black light that attracted mosquitoes. They were electrocuted as they flew through the grid. The product worked perfectly when being tested; however, no testing was ever done in the lab or by the regulatory authorities, or by us under live conditions as we couldn't buy mosquitoes to use for testing.

As it turned out, the bodies of the insects would carbonize and then drop to the bottom and build up an electrical carbon path between the two wires. When that happened, it created a continuous electrical arc between the two wires and a path across the plastic. This caught them on fire, and since they were hanging in homes and barns, they could and did catch fire and destroyed a couple of barns. Since this was our main product, to quit manufacturing them would have put us out of business, but to continue would mean we would be risking people's lives and property.

I called a meeting with all the management and told them that while financially we could accept the liability of a few lawsuits if we were to continue manufacturing and also that we could stay in business while working to solve the problem. But in the meantime, we were risking people's lives and property. A truly great company is a company made up of people with moral character. Early on, I learned you can only find out if you have people of that caliber when it's really crunch time.

I explained that since there was no way we would deliberately sell a product with the chance of harming someone, I wanted to recall all the product that we had sold. I also pointed out that in doing this, we would most likely go broke, and they would lose their jobs. I asked them, once we start the recall, will you stay with me until it's finished with the high likelihood that you probably won't get paid all your salaries? Meg Retinger, the office manager, and Bill Maples, the COO, did not hesitate. Their first statement was, we are wasting time; get everyone on the phone, and let's get these things back in. All of these people stayed with me until I sold the company in 2005, after 37 years in business. Meg Retinger went on to run two companies for me and is still COO of one of them.

As luck would have it, GE had just come out with a plastic called Lexan that was arc resistant. We quickly changed the grid to this plastic, found a company that sold "flies" in trays, and we now had an in-house testing system to confirm the safety of the product. At least there was a funny part to this – when the fly trays would be accidentally overturned, we would have thousands of them flying around the plant. We survived and went on to be the largest manufacturer of this product in the U.S.

Randy lived through this and later started his sales career marketing this product around the world. I truly believe that he learned a very valuable lesson from this. The lesson is fairly simple – find great, honest people and do what it takes to keep them, and secondly, do not let making money get in

the way of doing the right thing. When Randy started his own company, he
went through a similar product development problem.

His product problem wouldn't kill anyone, but I remember him
driving to the Greyhound bus station at night picking up defective products,
repairing them, and the next night shipping them back out. He had learned
that taking care of your customer is the only way to build a lasting business.

Having done the right thing at Fi-Shock, several of our customers
appreciated what we had done and actually placed larger orders and at the
same time prepaid us to help us stay alive. Unfortunately, I'm not sure this
kind of customer relationship still exists today.

I hope any aspiring young entrepreneur will not follow the "profits at any
cost" path that is being used today by a lot of larger companies. Some will
make products that they know are dangerous and simply keep selling them
as long as their accountants and legal departments tell them that the "cost of
death" isn't as big as the profits.

NEVER PASS UP A GOOD OPPORTUNITY

If a business owner has stockholders, its first obligation is to earn as
much profit as possible for them, but this has to be tempered with a concern
for the employees, who after all, are the company.

In the early 1980s, the beginning of the Asian invasion started in the
U.S. and worldwide. Due to cheap labor, many companies in the U.S. started
outsourcing their manufacturing to Asian companies. I fought this in every
way I could, but it was a losing battle. Our competitors began buying their
product at one half of what it was costing us to manufacture in the U.S. We
went from 300 employees to 100 in less than two years. We were effectively
forced out of the electronic bug killer business.

We still had our cattle containment systems, so we decided that we would
give this our full focus and at the same time keep our employees, who were
really our family. This required adding new products and efficiencies to reach
our goals. We thought this could be done utilizing companies that I had done

business with in the past to manufacture transformers and capacitors and for mold building and die casting.

We started getting notified daily that these suppliers were no longer making these products but were outsourcing from Korea, Taiwan, and China and could still sell us products, but lead times would be two or three months. The killing blow was when we attempted to have a new mold made for a plastic part we needed and found our supplier had gone out of business.

We knew that we could keep our existing employees busy by letting them do those jobs that could not be outsourced, such as injection molding, final assembly of electronics, and any high freight items that no matter what the labor rate was, the Asians could not be competitive. Our challenge was, we had to dramatically increase our sales in these types of products.

Unfortunately, today we do not have the basic framework for manufacturing in this country. Contrary to popular hopes and dreams, it will take years to rebuild our infrastructure to once again be the manufacturer to the world. It takes years to train tool and die makers and billions to recreate the basic supply chains that manufacturers require. We had to either join the crowd and start outsourcing or go out of business, and all our employees would lose their jobs.

People now talk about the China connection. It did not start out that way. In the 1980s, our first outsourcing was in Korea.

I will take a break in this story to say I have great hope that most of our country's manufacturing will come back to the U.S. It won't be because of tariffs or laws but will be due to the general nature of business.

I had a friend that was an ex-buyer for Western Auto. In the process of purchasing for them, he learned the ins and outs of outsourcing and how to get the best prices from the most reliable sources. He loved doing this and quit Western Auto and became an independent agent for companies in the U.S.; Fi-Shock, Inc. became one of them.

Each time I visited Korea on a purchasing trip, we would stay at the

Chosun Hotel in Seoul. We usually had dinner in the same restaurant that gave us a clear view of one of the city's busiest intersections. The first year we were there, all we saw were bicycles. Within a year, motorbikes started showing up, and by my fifth trip, we started seeing a small number of automobiles.

Over time, we began to notice there were continuous price increases as the shortage of labor and the large amounts of exports began pushing up the cost of labor. One night a group of us sat around the hotel lobby debating what these changing conditions meant for our business, so we developed a new purchasing concept. We decided to simply follow the bicycle. In other words, we could tell from the progression of transportation in Asian countries when prices would go up.

Our solution was to start transferring our purchases to Taiwan as they were just starting their ability to manufacture. You guessed it, first trip we saw all bicycles. The Taiwanese learned quickly. We all stayed at the Brother Hotel in Taipei looking out on the main thoroughfare. Within the next two trips, motorbikes took over, and by the fourth trip, cars were moving in. At this point we moved out and headed for China.

There is no longer cheap labor in Korea and Taiwan, and the cost of labor in China has increased dramatically over the last decade. Cheap labor is no longer our excuse for buying imports. Our reality in the U.S. is that we have to rebuild our infrastructure and to do that requires a dramatic shift in our view of education and its importance in the training of the future technicians it will take to compete in the 21st century.

Randy has watched this all develop over the years, and I believe he has an inside view of what it will take to bring the jobs home. It involves heavier emphasis on technical and trade schools and putting those schools closer to the student so that they can get the training they need.

I think that I was no different than any other father. When I started my first company, I took it for granted that I would build it and eventually pass it on to my son. I now believe that Randy understood me better than I knew myself. By his mid-20s, he probably came to the realization that I was the type of fellow who would probably have a hard time turning his company over and letting his son do his own thing. He was right I kept this company until I was 67 and by then Randy had a very successful company. Our product line would not have fit into his long-term plans, so I decided it was probably time to sell.

The following is not a father/son story, but it is relevant. In 2005 I contacted an agent to sell the company. We were a very successful, solid company with a history of continuous growth. I was having a hard time leaving my people, many of whom I had worked with for over 30 years, but at 67 and having had a heart attack at 60, I felt that the time had come.

My agent brought a potential buyer to us, and still undecided if I wanted to sell, I had the agent bring the buyer to a restaurant at the airport. We met and the potential buyer said that he was very interested in buying our company. I told him I was not sure I wanted to sell, but I would tell him what I want for it. I wrote the price out on a napkin and handed it to him and said this is non-negotiable. We won't talk again until I see the money in the bank. I gave him my CFO's name and told him he could only talk to him. I then went back and told my CFO, never mention this to me again until you give me the wire transfer number and the money is on its way.

Sounds ridiculous, but I knew I would probably change my mind if I got involved in the negotiations. It worked and we received 14 times EBITDA (Earnings Before Interest, Taxes, Depreciation and Amortization) for the company, which was unheard of at that time when most companies were going for less than 8 times EBITDA. Most importantly, our stockholders received a great return on their money.

During the 37 years that I had this company, I rarely took a vacation, and when I did I usually returned home early. My wife was so used to this that after I would leave, she would take a picture of herself with her arm out pretending to have me there. This became quite a hit with her friends as she was always sending them pictures of our vacations with the phantom "Tom."

The week after we sold the business, my wife insisted that we take our very first two-week vacation. My son and his wife went with us to an island in the Caribbean. After the first few days, I knew I was in trouble. I had never known a time I wasn't working or thinking of new ideas for business.

Before the week was over, I knew I couldn't do it. By the second week, I was happy again as I had come up with several ideas for a new business. I didn't anticipate the one that I would eventually buy.

The new business centered on a local company doing colon cancer research. I met with the owner and shortly thereafter with their board and decided to buy the company. I contacted several of my friends and offered them the opportunity to invest. They did, and we formed a new company *EDP Biotech*.

I had never been involved with a company that didn't produce products and that didn't have sales and income. I knew absolutely nothing about the medical industry but simply assumed that it would be like any other business. I asked a friend who had been involved in similar types of products and he said, "Tom, it looks like it has potential. If it hits, it will be big and also be very valuable in saving lives from colon of cancer." He went on to be one of the company's first investors.

I will never forget my friend's first statement, "This is a gamble. We can be in the market in a year or it may take many years." At present, it has taken 13 years and has morphed considerably since the first product concept. We have now developed a multiplex test named Colon Plex that will predict early stages colon of cancer from a blood test with a high degree of accuracy. Along the way there have been many setbacks, but the end result has been worth it.

Once again, the lesson for entrepreneurs is that one's early expectations are rarely accomplished, but if you stay with an idea through all its ups and downs, most of the time you will win.

I always tell people that are working with me that when they want to give up, think in these terms: "If you are climbing a high mountain and really get tired on the way up, just start taking a step at a time, and eventually you will get to the top and be much happier by having done so. Going down the hill and reaping the rewards will soon make you forget the hardships of going up."

One of the most valuable lessons I have learned over the years is that businesses rarely end up the way one expects nor is the end result set in stone. As an entrepreneur goes along, he/she must positively consider any opportunity that presents itself. In 2008 after three years in the cancer research, I was tired of running a company that ate money without producing income. I challenged the people working with me to come up with something that would create an income stream, and it had to be big enough that I could get excited. I wanted a product that had an unlimited market potential and that could be sold worldwide.

We thought the development of this product idea would require extensive research, but instead it happened overnight. To get some ideas started, I asked some employees to meet at a friend's house for a brainstorming session. When the meeting started, I asked each participant if they had any experience outside the cancer research field. One of them said he did some early work in the DNA field when he was with a lab in Ireland.

The meeting continued for a while, and after a few more beers, we came up with all kinds of ideas, but none of them struck me as winners. About this time another employee came in and said he had just stepped in a pile of dog waste. He was very angry. He used a few words that are not printable, but the rant was about what he would do to the person who did not pick up after his dog. This anger restarted the conversation around how you would catch this person. I don't remember now who came up with the solution. Once the conversation went in this direction, it wasn't an hour before we had the basis of what we thought was a new company. The business concept was to develop a pet waste management product based on DNA technology.

The following week we worked on determining who our customers would be. We knew that for the idea to work, dogs had to be in a contained area and be in large concentrations. We did a survey of apartment complexes as to the number that were dog-friendly. It was simple from there. Statistics showed that over 40% of dog owners never pick up after their pet. Assuming an apartment complex had 100 dogs, that meant that 80 droppings a day or 2400 a month had to be walked around or picked up. It is very expensive for the apartment management and very emotional for the responsible dog owners to have to contend with this. We named the new company BioPet Vet Laboratories.

We had a company name, but we felt that this would not mean anything to anyone, and we would be explaining the company through most of the sales calls. After reviewing hundreds of names, I suggested that the product should be named for what it was without being too ridiculous. We finally settled on *PooPrints*. This has been proven to be a perfect name as it's catchy and states what we are doing. It also creates a lot of interest in the media. *PooPrints* has been featured in *USA Today*, *Good Morning America*, "Jay Leno Show," *NY Times*, *London Times*, *Washington Post*, *Chicago Tribune*, just to name a few. We were also the only company that I know of that was solicited by "Shark Tank" to present on their show. We did the filming and were on schedule to air the next year, but by airing time we had received publicity all over the world and no longer had a new product.

Branding is very important. In the beginning Randy's company was called Radio Fence, then changed to Radio Systems. This did not represent what he was selling. Ultimately, Randy changed the product name to PetSafe which not only defined the product but conveyed a compelling message to the consumer.

Our goal was to sell the program to a minimum of one apartment in a minimum of 30 states by the end of the first year. During that time, we had to perfect our tracking system and enlarge our DNA analysis, so it could be done on a large scale. By the second year, we had signed properties in all 50 states, and better yet, the company was profitable. We now have over 3000 multi-family properties using our products and are adding a new one every hour. We also have gone international and have a complete borough of London, England using the product and customers in Israel, Canada, Mexico, Singapore, and Australia.

The lesson I hope to convey to budding entrepreneurs is that one never knows what direction a company will take. It most likely will not have any resemblance to your first ideas. Also, continually watch for opportunities and do not hesitate to try new things.

BioPet is now a multi-million dollar company in sales for its flagship product *PooPrints*. The company is also introducing a number of new additional related products.

Although we know what the company looks like now, there is a strong possibility that the company will morph many times in the future.

What has this got to do with my son? I believe genes dictate one's life, and in Randy's company, he has posted this directive for his associates to follow:

"Try a lot of things and keep what works."

SECTION II

RANDY DEVELOPS HIS OWN STYLE

Watching Randy develop his own business style has given me great joy. However, Randy may not agree, for in his mind I made him learn "the hard way." Remember, I believe that we have become what we are because of our experiences and what we were yesterday.

My father used to say, "If the sun catches a man in bed, he's not worth the powder and lead to blow him up." From a very early age, this is the work ethic Randy has always embraced.

Randy never wanted to waste time, and the day he finished college, he came to my office and said, "Dad, you promised me a job, and I'm ready to go to work." I said, "Son, graduation day is not until next week, and you can start then." He replied, "I've done the work and can't see any reason to wait, and I don't want to lose the time. I know I've done it and don't need a piece of paper to make it official." I said to him, "You are definitely my son."

As has always been the case, Randy really downplayed his early job successes. He quickly developed new business in England, Saudi Arabia, and Venezuela. He developed an innovative system for obtaining leads in foreign countries that I still use today. The fact is, learning is not a one-way street. Over the years, I've incorporated many ideas that Randy pioneered into my businesses.

When Randy frequently says he's cheap, what he really means is he is frugal. Being an entrepreneur and building businesses make saving money a necessity. In Randy's words –

"You can't get to a dollar without going through a penny."

Even when my company was growing and money wasn't much of a problem, Randy was always mindful of my commandment that we were operating with the shareholders' money. We were developing a business in England and staying in a London hotel. Randy needed to write and prepare a multi-page sales presentation. The hotel charged ten cents per page to print the presentation. Randy noticed that the hotel provided faxes free. I assume the hotel thought that most faxes were one page. Randy went to the lobby and faxed the full presentation to himself, thereby saving the printing cost. It made his day.

Sometime earlier when Randy began his first international sales work, he had been on the road for about a month. He and I were to meet in Paris, France where we had a trade show to attend. I checked into a hotel near the show site expecting Randy to meet me there that night. He was coming from Italy, so I knew he was supposed to arrive around 4:00 in the afternoon. The train station was on the other side of Paris. He didn't show up that night, and since there were no cell phones then, I spent an anxious night worrying about him. The next morning I went down to get coffee and found a spot facing the street. I saw this person walking down the street toward the hotel. It was Randy, looking beat and tired. When he came in he was holding up a dime. I asked, "What's the dime for?" He replied, "I ran out of money and had to walk here, but I kept the dime for an absolute emergency." Randy had been given an expense allowance and wasn't about to ask for any more.

We worked trade shows together in Venezuela, Puerto Rico, France, England, and Germany.

Before Randy became my star salesman, he began working in our manufacturing plant running a stamping press. He was obsessed with setting production targets, increasing production each day, and beating his own records. Constant improvement has been a life lesson well-learned. Whether it's business growth, beating his best time running, or climbing the highest mountain, Randy is continually looking for his next challenge. While well-deserved, Randy has always avoided praise, but now that his successes have been so great, I can admit I'm proud of his accomplishments. Nevertheless, I still expect him to beat his last record.

Today, Randy's business ventures and interests are widely varied. His greatest business success has been the development and growth of Radio

Systems Corporation. The company has become the world's leading dog and cat products supplier.

The content in the following chapters reflects the early years of Radio Systems and has been paraphrased from Randy's personal journals.

Randy started working for me in 1979. A lot of things had changed since I started my first business in 1961.

Of course, we had a new president, Jimmy Carter. It was the year that we had an oil crisis. President Carter thought we could save our way out of the crisis by cutting back thermostats. That didn't work. Inflation shot up to 11.2%. Businesses were paying as high as 18% for borrowed money. Due to the ever-increasing interest rates, we ceased putting out annual price schedules for our product; rather we would put one out with prices escalating every quarter. This created a false sense of growth; we had 20+% growth without doing anything.

It was a crazy year worldwide. Russia invaded Afghanistan, Margaret Thatcher was elected Prime minister of the UK, and ominously, Khomeini in Iran took 63 American hostages, which eventually ruined Jimmy Carter's second bid for the presidency, thus making the way for Ronald Reagan. Oil reached $24 per barrel for the first time.

Movies had some great hits, *Rocky II, Alien, The Amityville Horror, The Deer Hunter,* and *Star Trek.* "All My Children," "M*A*S*H," and "The Price is Right" were the top TV shows. On the light side, the first British nudist beach was opened in Brighton, England.

Wages had more than tripled to an average of $17,500. Gas skyrocketed from 36 cents in 1961 to 86 cents. The big fear was that it could actually reach $1, and no one could afford to drive. The cost of a home had advanced dramatically to $54,000.

The value of a dollar then is worth $3.64 in 2018. Note that the item we complain the most about, gas, has increased at less than the rate of inflation, while home costs have increased six times.

The costs of college grew by 260% compared to all consumer goods at 120%. This has been detrimental to our country as a whole and created unnecessary debt for students. The obvious question is: Why?

CHAPTER 4

WORKING WITH DAD –
THE EARLY LESSONS

I graduated with honors from the University of Tennessee in Knoxville at the ripe old age of 19 in 1979. I can honestly say that it wasn't a case of brilliance but more my impatience to get on with life. It's fair to say that this trait still persists! In fact, this impatience, for better or worse, still permeates my business today. However, the part that I'm most proud of is that I paid my own way through college, being in debt to my father $440 upon graduation, a debt I soon paid off. I hear parents talk about not being able to afford college for their children or students saying that four-year degrees are impossible and that it really takes five years these days. I don't have a lot of sympathy for either.

Still, I have to give credit to my father for giving me the opportunity to work. When I was 6, he gave me a job working on a packaging assembly line. At a $1 per hour, I felt rich! To those thinking of violations to child labor laws, please note that Dad paid me out of his pocket. A few years later, I got "promoted" to the electronic assembly line. I learned more about time and motion studies then than I did at the university but didn't even know it was a science until many years later. The ladies that I worked with were unbelievably fast at repetitive, meticulous jobs. Every tray of parts was carefully positioned for ease and quick access. Every hand movement was practiced for optimum efficiency. Everyone started precisely at 7:00 a.m. and took very exacting breaks. To get up from your station any other time would cause parts to pile up on your one side and shut everyone down on the other side. Obviously, it just wasn't done. I have great respect for an assembly line and those who work on it. They are a perfect, natural team.

On the assembly line, if one job or person was a little slow, others quickly adjusted to add a bit more of the assembly to their station. It was an automatic, self-balancing process. There were no industrial engineers hovering over them. So much of that work and almost all other forms of work are simple, common sense. And no one knows how better to react, and adjust than the person on the front line doing the work. I have realized that it's only when people are instructed to blindly obey directives from someone not directly involved that the processes get complicated, usually inefficient, and most importantly, frustrating and demoralizing for those doing it. Today, my operating philosophy continues to be to give responsibility and key decision-making to the front lines as much as possible.

By age 14, I had made the big time – minimum wage and a legal employee. It was a heady time! I took advantage of opportunity every chance I got – summers, holiday breaks, and the occasional weekend. I also got to move on to more manly pursuits such as running a riveting machine. I was always challenged to set the new "world record" for riveting insulators to a metal flange. I would set a new record and proudly announce it to my father. Unfortunately, in a matter of days my Dad would inform me that so and so on another shift broke my record. It was a cycle that repeated endlessly. But I never met my nemesis and intend one day to extract a confession from Dad that he really didn't exist.

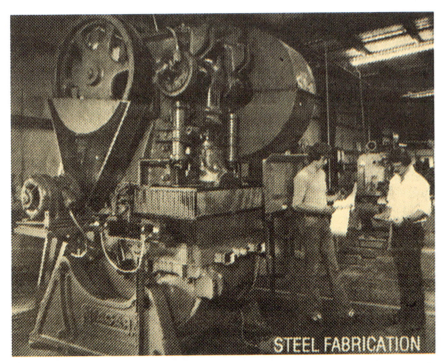

STEEL FABRICATION

I'll share another favorite job though I'm not sure of my moral justification for sharing it other than I just like telling it. Sorry. Another important business at Fi-Shock in those days was the manufacture of steel fence posts. The process consisted of cutting rebar into 48" lengths, welding a razor-sharp flange onto them, dipping a rack of them into paint, then removing them from the rack and using a metal twist tie to bundle 25 at time. Due to the fumes from the paint, it had to be an outside job and was done rain or shine in 100-degree summer days and freezing winter days. The efficiency of the process was gauged by the welder's speed, a job I loved though it was probably fairly hazardous. Bundling was also challenging. It consisted of picking up bundles of posts weighing around 30 pounds with flanges on each end and covered in wet, silver paint. Throughout the bundling process, one's hands would be half silver and half red from the blood from the inevitable cuts.

For a teenager, it was considered a man's profession (though there were on occasion some very strong women at a few positions). The best part was the sense of accomplishment that was immediate and consistent. You knew at the end of the day what you accomplished and that you could be proud of putting in a good day's work. You didn't have to wait years to find out if you made the right decision nor were you dependent on someone else to tell you that you did a good job. You knew. In spite of the demanding work and maybe simply because of it, it was very satisfying. This was a lesson that would follow me throughout my work career.

Somewhere in these stories is an attempt to share with you the lessons I learned about work. Job and self-satisfaction don't come from what job you do, but how well you do it. You may not be changing the world, but if you feel you've given 100% and done your best, there is something extremely satisfying and enriching in your efforts. Thus, no matter what responsibilities one may have, the same opportunity for being content with one's work is always available.

By the time I started at the University of Tennessee, I was working in plastics running injection molding machines. I had the weekend shift getting in 24 hours by working 7:00 p.m. to 7:00 a.m. Saturday night and Sunday night. It was a good job, and often when the machines were running the right mix, I could actually get about 20 minutes studying in per hour if I balanced everything just right. I must admit though that staying awake during my Monday morning business law class was difficult. However, what I didn't learn in business law and now have to pay $300 per hour for, I did learn in

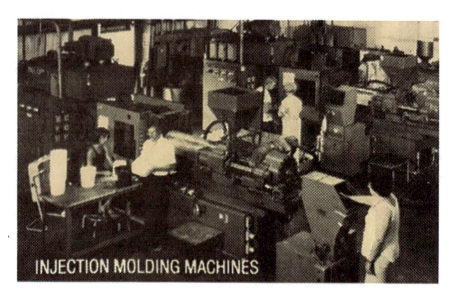

INJECTION MOLDING MACHINES

working with plastics. In the early years of Radio Systems, a little of this plastics knowledge probably contributed to some of the early product designs and eventually to being able to afford to pay those attorneys.

During summers and on holidays, I worked for a second company my father had, U.S. Distributing, the forerunner of Saco Distributing. As with Saco later, it was a sales-driven company with a few salesmen, one being my mother who drove a van around to feed and farm supply stores selling out of the truck. Both Mom and Dad trained me. Mom was very meticulous and knew her product inside and out, always giving the customer an overwhelming amount of product knowledge.

However, my father was and is still the best salesman I've ever known. He didn't bother much with the details of the product. When training me, he'd let me go in and give my pitch first. I'd have all the words right, knew the product well, but still wouldn't get to first base. Then Dad would find something to break the ice, bringing up a possible mutual acquaintance or a perceptively-chosen subject sure to spark interest. Before long, he would have a huge order.

I now know his secret. He could meet a stranger, and the person immediately became his best, lifelong friend. The customer could see it in his eyes and his smile. Who wouldn't want to buy from him? Even when they really didn't need the product, they would buy. It's a trait that I still try to emulate with some, but not equal, success. And you can't fake it; Dad never did. He truly was excited to meet people and had a genuine and immediate interest in them.

Years later when I was working as a salesman for Fi-Shock and traveling through Oklahoma, I stopped at an out of the way farm distributor in Enid, Oklahoma. When I introduced myself, the buyer asked if I was Tom Boyd's son. When I said I was, I was given a warm and welcome reception. He talked about Dad as if they were long-time friends. I asked how I knew him and he replied that Dad had called on him once eight years before!

As a salesman for U.S. Distributing, I was given all the choice territories establishing new accounts in Arkansas and Missouri (I'm being facetious).

I soon learned how to handle rejection because I got a tremendous amount of practice. One two-week trip that consisted of ten cold calls a day netted exactly zero sales until the very last day. I just didn't quite have Dad's talent. In my defense, I do think that the store owners had a hard time taking a 16-year-old from Tennessee with a van full of product as a serious vendor.

As a result of the weekend plastic manufacturing shifts and the summers selling product for U.S. Distributing, I managed to pay my way through UT. I never went to a football game or other event, lived at home, and probably missed out on the fun, social life that others experienced. However, I do believe the self-discipline was a healthy experience, and believe I learned at least as much, if not more, from the act of paying my way through than I did in class itself.

FI-SHOCK – MY OWN WORK CAREER BEGINS

Upon graduation, my father gave me a fabulous job as director of international marketing for his Fi-Shock company. The company had revenues of $4 million ($13 million/2018) at the time and grew to $8 million ($26 million/2018), solely on the strength of a dynamic new product, the electronic bug killer. Popularly known as "bug zappers," they consisted of an ultraviolet light that attracted bugs to a metal grid that then electrocuted them. I had an office with a great 21st-floor view, a job working for a dynamic, growing company, and was on top of the world in spite of a beginning salary of only $12,000 ($38,000/2018).

As early as high school, I wanted to be involved in international affairs. My highest personal, lifetime goal was to one day be appointed to a high diplomatic position and then work my way up to secretary of state. A position in international sales was a perfect opportunity. And, being 19 and single, I had the key qualification for a job which required extensive travel far away and for long periods of time. I was flexible and didn't have anything requiring me to stay at home.

We generated international sales leads at trade shows. There were also services that the Commerce Department provided to generate leads. In a few cases, I would simply call the U.S. commercial attaché a few weeks before I was to arrive and ask if we could meet. I would arrive, discuss our need for a distributor, and they would make calls and arrange appointments. "Hello, this is the commercial attaché with the U.S. Embassy" was an effective way to get the buyer's attention in many smaller countries! In some cases, the attaché or their assistants were extremely helpful. Once in Ecuador, the assistant not only made all the appointments but also took two days driving me to each appointment and acting as a translator when needed.

I served in this position for two years but only with moderate success. While I managed to acquire many good distributors, our horrendous product failure rate with the bug killers made every customer a one-time sell. In the process, I managed to visit over 35 countries including nearly all in Western Europe and South and Central America. Fi-Shock began having financial difficulties in 1981, and all international sales activities were discontinued. However, I am still thankful for the experience.

Today Radio Systems is a very international company, with over 400 indirect workers assembling product for us in China, another 50 in Mexico, distribution and sales offices in the United Kingdom and Canada, packaging in nine languages, and sales to over 30 countries around the world. Some small part of this global influence can be traced back to those experiences in the early Fi-Shock days as director of international marketing.

After the international sales efforts were discontinued, I was first made regional sales manager for the Midwest. I lived in Chicago and called on accounts such as Sears, Montgomery Ward, Payless-Cashways, and Creative Publishing (once big in catalog showrooms). After a year I was promoted to vice president of sales for the electronic bug killer product line. During this time I worked probably 30 trade shows a year and managed a national network of sales reps, some of whom helped Radio Systems get started years later. It was during this period that I learned the basic skills and knowledge needed to create a national sales and marketing organization, keys to my ability to successfully start Radio Systems eight years later.

THE ORIGINAL SACO: SETTING OUT ALONE

Many have asked what "Saco" stands for, and according to the state of Tennessee's records, it stands for "Southern Agricultural Co-operatives." It's an awkward and incongruous name. Why was it picked? I should give you a little history.

In 1983, an inventor came to Fi-Shock with an invention that detected tornadoes, or so he said. It was a fairly simple device, which consisted of a barometer and an alarm. The theory was that a tornado or conditions for one would not exist without a sudden drop in barometric pressure. When the pressure got to a certain point set by the consumer (28.5 was recommended), an alarm would sound.

Growing up in East Tennessee, I had no appreciation for the dangers of tornadoes. However, my father did, having grown up in West Tennessee. He thought it was a great idea. Unfortunately, Fi-Shock was not in a position to develop new products at the time.

In fact, it was a very difficult time for Fi-Shock. The company had lost lots of money in the electronic bug killer business and that August was in the process of filing Chapter 11. Most people would have looked at the financial situation of the company and said it should simply close up. However, my father was not a quitter. He also felt a strong sense of responsibility to all of his stockholders, those who had trusted in him with their investments, and he didn't want to let them down. While those days weren't pleasant, it was a very valuable learning experience. One of the most important lessons was learning first-hand that if one is determined, no one can put you out of business. You must emotionally give up in order to fail. If one can take the stress and pressure that comes with a bad financial situation, one can always persevere.

Fi-Shock's business difficulties taught me many practical lessons about how to finance and run a business with little or no cash. It seemed that every day there was a new crisis, but at the end of the day, I could go home and know that in the morning Dad would have a solution. These were lessons that proved very valuable in later years. When Radio Systems had its inevitable difficult times, as any company will, these experiences at Fi-Shock reminded me that there was always a way to overcome as long as we persisted and didn't give up.

In this context, an opportunity presented itself. Dad gave me permission to toy with the storm alert product. After many hours of tinkering in the evenings, I cobbled together different parts of Fi-Shock raw materials in order to assemble a working prototype of the storm alert. In early October, I took a week vacation and went to Missouri to show my product. In the first week, I sold 450 Storm Alert products at $16 each. Since they only cost me $7 to make in parts, I assumed I was rich! With $9 in gross margin per unit times 450 units, I had grossed over $4,000 for the week. That week confirmed what I knew all along – Dad had been underpaying me (in spite of titles, I was still at around $16,000 a year). If I were on my own, I could finally achieve my true worth. Unfortunately, this was by far the best week I would ever have.

The next week I quit Fi-Shock and went out on my own full of confidence and excitement. My father had a good man in the wings, and I was confident he could replace me ably and quickly. My leaving also reduced payroll at Fi-Shock. So on October 1, 1983 at age 23, I was off on my own.

The first order of business was to open a checking account. I went down to the bank and was filling out the forms for opening the account when they asked me what I wanted to put on the checks for the name of the company. Naming the company hadn't even occurred to me! Since we had only one product, the Storm Alert, I mumbled to just put "Storm Alert" on them or maybe "Storm Alert Company." That didn't sound too good, so the banker and I agreed on an acronym for the company name, "Saco."

Assembling the product proved to be a challenge. We made them in my best friend (and partner) Cary Neely's basement with an assortment of friends and acquaintances. We quickly invested in tooling (by buying on terms) and created a very nice-looking product in an attractive package. The typical work week involved driving 12 to 14 hours to the Midwest Sunday afternoon, selling product Monday through Friday out of the back of the car, driving home late Friday night to arrive in the wee hours Saturday morning, and then crash assembly sessions all weekend to build enough product for the following week.

The good news was that I could sell the product in sixes or dozens to Western Autos, drug stores, and small hardware stores throughout Arkansas, Missouri, Alabama, Mississippi, Oklahoma, and Kansas. I would usually end up with one dealer per town by promising them an exclusive for that town and adding them to our local advertising campaign (usually a handful of late night commercials in the local market, e.g. Jonesboro, Arkansas).

I thought I was always frugal when traveling for Fi-Shock, sleeping on trains while traveling through Europe and always staying at very inexpensive local hotels. But I learned how to take it to the next level when starting Saco. I found that most of the cheap hotels I would stay at would not get completely booked, and there would be a room available as early as 6:00 a.m. So I could sleep in the car one night, check in early and get cleaned up, then use the room again that night. Two nights for the price of one! I still remember certain nights; in particular, a very long, cold night during a snowstorm in Kansas City. Meals consisted of a cheeseburger and water, and I would look disgustedly upon those that would waste money on such indulgences as French fries that had no nutritional value. Not having to sleep in the car is definitely one of the perks that comes with running a more established business, and I still appreciate these luxuries (and still consider them as such).

After about three months in business, things began to go badly. First, I had counted on factoring our receivables with a friend of my father's (a process of selling one's invoices to a third party at a discount, usually 5%). This person had a change of heart and decided not to do it.

More importantly, after about six months of setting up dealers, not a single one ever reordered a sale. In fact, to my knowledge, no one ever sold a unit. I'm sure someone did, I'm just unaware of it. I soon realized that one day I would run out of small towns and new dealers. And, another valuable lesson – one cannot operate indefinitely without repeat customers.

SACO IS REBORN

In January of 1984, Saco was having problems getting parts, and it appeared I would be stuck in town for a week. Not wanting to lose a week of valuable sales time, I remembered that Fi-Shock had some small farm stores in Georgia that I used to call on when I was Fi-Shock's sales manager. So I talked Dad into selling me some electric fencing product on consignment for one week. I'd pick up the product on a Saturday and return the product plus payment for what I'd sold on the following Saturday. I rented a Dodge Maxi van from Budget for $330 and headed off, hoping I could cover at least the rental cost and my expenses.

I ended that first week with $2,700 in sales ($6,588/2018) and a gross margin of $900 ($2,196/2018), which was enough to cover expenses and put a $400-$500 ($1,220) profit in the bank (figuratively speaking). Then, when Saco's product was again available, I went back to Arkansas to sell Storm Alerts.

Then a funny thing began happening. The stores that I sold electric fencing to in Georgia started calling wanting more products. I had a brilliant insight – wow, products that retailers actually sold and needed more of was a business opportunity that had some real potential!

By May I had made three trips through Georgia and decided it was time to buy a Dodge Maxi van of my own. It was a white van with no air or radio and was driven up to 550,000 miles before it was retired. Also in May I hired and trained my first salesman for Saco.

During the summer of 1984, I gradually spent more and more time with the farm supply side of the business and realized it was time to liquidate the Storm Alert side. I found a young couple in Chattanooga who was willing to pay me $14,000, in installments to buy that part of the business and all the Storm Alert molds and inventory. My friend and partner, Cary Neely, accepted a small amount of cash for his 40% stake.

Unfortunately, they got to keep the name Saco, Inc. Since all my stationary said Saco on it, I tried to incorporate under the name Saco

Distributing, but the state of Tennessee wouldn't allow it. So I came up with an official name that allowed me to use the same initials. Thus, the official name "Southern Agricultural Co-operatives" was created, and I could keep my stationery! Such expense considerations were all important in those days.

For the first six months of the new Saco, I had no catalogs. I wrote orders with mimeographed order forms and used carbon paper to make copies. Using a special glue, I made my own order pads. I would go into the store with a big 18-quart plastic bucket, but you only pay for what you see. Then I'd pour my samples out on the counter. It was self-effacing, broke the ice, and buyers loved it. When they heard that the lead time for delivery was about five minutes (the time it would take to go out to the van to bring it in), they were sold.

Thus, for those salesmen who have plodded through to this point, beware from whence I came. I have little sympathy for salesman who can't make a sales call if they are missing a catalog sheet or even a sample, let alone some other lesser excuse. It's certainly nice to have the peripheral support material but not essential to be successful.

We were also fairly famous for our "office," if you want to call it that. It was a dilapidated, unroadworthy, blackened over-the-road tractor-trailer with half-flat tires. We backed it up to an unused portion of Fi-Shock's loading dock. My Dad and I spent several weekends building an office on the inside which was quite nice, complete with sheet rock, hanging ceiling, and carpet. I paid the phone company for an extra line into Fi-Shock and then ran an extension cord and a phone line down a plastic pipe from the building into the trailer. While we did own our own phone line, I probably to this day still owe Fi-Shock for the electricity. It was surprisingly nice inside with air conditioning and very modern Scandinavian furniture (the kind you assemble, which we did). We did miss windows, however, and it could get quite cold on winter mornings and quite hot on summer afternoons in spite of the in-wall heater/air conditioner.

By 1989, Southern Agriculture Co-operatives (Saco) had ten salesmen covering 2,500 farm stores from Bellevue, Washington to Bangor, Maine to

Kissimmee, Florida to Amarillo, Texas. Approximately 1,000 of the accounts I had cold-called and set up personally. It was hard work calling on eight to ten stores a day, five days a week, getting home late on Fridays, and then unloading, doing paperwork, and re-loading on Saturdays. However, it was a profitable, steady business.

Most importantly, I learned a lot of valuable lessons. One of the most important was a lasting appreciation of the value of the customer. Making ten cold calls a day in hopes to get one or two to buy $100 or $200 worth of product makes one appreciate every customer, no matter how small. It took eight years to save up $26,000 in net equity, staying in the absolutely cheapest hotels I could find and with daily meal budgets not exceeding $12. Economy was a necessity that became a habit and the realization today that every successful business is a nickel and dime business no matter how large it is.

The following is Randy's story of how he started Radio Fence Systems. I believe his story is a "must read" for anyone desiring to start a company or believing they want to be an entrepreneur.
It is quite detailed, but in business, the devil is in the details.

CHAPTER 5

AN IDEA THAT LAUNCHED A COMPANY

George H.W. Bush was president in 1989.
The value of a dollar then is worth $2.06 in 2018.

Sometime during 1989, I forget exactly when, a manager at a Gold Kist Store in Andersonville, South Carolina asked me if I could get the Invisible Fence product for him. I will always remember his statement – "It doesn't matter what they cost, I can sell as many as you can get." That would be music to the ears of any much-traveled peddler, and it definitely was to mine.

With this incentive, I humbly called Invisible Fence. I was passed around for what seemed like 30 minutes before I finally got a lady who said she was the assistant to the vice president of sales. I explained that while we weren't Sears, we had about two thousand farm supply stores serviced by ten salesmen, and we thought we could sell some of their product. Being a salesman, I expected them to respond eagerly to a new customer calling. However, instead the response was – "Your proposal is interesting. Why don't you put it in writing and mail it to our vice president, and maybe in six months to a year, he might get back with you?" I was frustrated and somewhat shocked. After spending so many years cold-calling and scrapping for customers, I couldn't imagine such arrogance to a potential customer!

I didn't write the letter "describing how I would like to buy." Instead, I decided to do some research. I had a friend and banker, Todd Birdwell, pull a Dun and Bradstreet report on them. It showed they had revenues of about $8 million. It also showed that they had a patent on their product, and it was due to expire in August of 1990. The potential sales and the prospect of being able to compete in the near future were encouraging.

I next called the local Invisible Fence dealer, (who it turned out was the younger brother of a good friend of my wife, Jenny). I explained to him that I wanted to sell the product but was rebuffed by his corporate headquarters. There was not a lot of love between this dealer and the parent company, a phenomenon I found out was pretty common. The dealer explained that the way Invisible Fence marketed their products was exclusively through franchise dealerships that made selling to a national distributor like Saco impossible. It would have been so much more convenient if Invisible Fence had courteously explained this when I had first called. I always remembered this lesson. Always treat anyone who calls you with respect and courtesy; you never know who you might inspire. I'm sure Invisible Fence would like to have their response to my call back!

In addition to information, the dealer provided me with samples and pricing. He was selling the complete, uninstalled system for about $850 and was paying $430 for it. I immediately broke it apart to get an idea of what it would cost to make. The receiver had components on it that I had never seen before in my limited experience with electric fencing electronics, something called surface mount circuitry. However, the transmitter looked much more comprehensible with its through-hole design. This one component of their system was sold separately at retail for about $425, and I could tell right away that there was only a fraction of that cost in the parts.

Enter Bill Franklin. The most underpaid, unheralded person in our company's history is Bill Franklin, a man I knew for many years prior to starting Radio Fence, who was a supplier of electronic components to my father's Fi-Shock company. He and his partner, Charles Ketron, the father of Jeff Ketron and shipping manager for Saco at the time, owned a company called Industrial Electronics. He not only knew sources of supply for nearly any electrical component but also had a great understanding of mechanical design and helped with many of our early designs. He knew everyone who was anyone in the electronics business in East Tennessee, and his introductions to them later were critical to our future success. Bill also provided the first product cost analysis.

I took a transmitter to him and as a favor asked him to dissect it and let me know the cost of the components. He came back the next day with a total bill of materials of around $13. This was a product Invisible Fence was charging over $400 for! I've since been fond of saying that at that moment, I had my only bit of brilliant inspiration, and that everything else afterwards was just hard work and surrounding myself with a lot of great people. And that one bit of brilliant inspiration was this – Somewhere between $13 and $400 a guy could sell a competitively priced product and make some money. Well, it may not have been that terribly brilliant, but it did turn out to be true.

BOOT STRAPPING 101:

A NEW COMPANY IS STARTED

Determining that there was a potential opportunity was the easy part. Now where to go from there? Again my electronics expert provided the answer. Not being an engineer and knowing none, I turned to him for suggestions. One of his customers had an electrical engineer who was known to do some moonlighting on occasion. Bill called him, and he agreed to meet with me. We met at a local restaurant one evening, and I explained the project and gave him some samples of the competition's product. He liked the idea, was confident he could do the design, and he agreed to make a proposal.

I no longer have a copy of the quote, but I remember it to be around $30,000 ($60,000/2018). Today, Radio Systems has an R&D budget over $4 million ($8 million/2018), so a $30,000 ($6,000/2018) expense doesn't sound like much. However, at the time it represented everything I owned and more. While my Saco company was a good, solid business, it had taken me eight years traveling five days a week six out of every eight weeks on a budget of $18 ($36) per night for a hotel and $10 ($20) per day for food to save up $26,000 ($52,000). Even that wasn't cash in hand, but it was what the balance sheet showed as the company's net worth. So, if I launched this new product, I would have to spend more to develop it than I had saved in eight years.

It might sound like an easy decision now, but it wasn't. I had a stable, secure business that supported my wife and two-year-old son, paid the mortgage, and allowed us to vacation occasionally. If we spent the money and couldn't get the product to work or it didn't sell, while I wouldn't be on the street, I would have blown my entire life's savings. I remember leaning back in my chair in the trailer discussing this with my office assistant, who was also my cousin. It was put up or shut up time. Ultimately I made the decision to proceed. As almost any entrepreneur will tell you, success is not about brilliance or luck. It's mostly about being willing to take a risk. We had just risked it all. But that was only the first step. After that it was about dogged determination. It was time to test our will.

While we were getting started on the product design, I got a call from a gentleman who had also been eyeing Invisible Fence's pending patent expiration (as were many others it turned out) and decided to start his own business. He had originally called my father looking for a source of transformers, and Dad had told him that I was also looking into the same business and that we should talk. We did discuss the possibility of splitting the R&D costs and starting some form of joint venture, him concentrating on installing dealers and me on the retail trade.

We spent considerable time discussing who would do what. In one scenario, my company was to pay for the tooling and transformer design, while the partner company was to contract for the electronic design. However, the more we explored the joint venture, the more complicated it got. In the end, we agreed that each company should pay for its own development. Just competing seemed like the best route. Though we are competitors, each company, true to its original plan, has focused on different market channels. As a result we have managed to maintain very friendly relations.

Meanwhile, the money flew out at an amazing rate, and there were many sleepless nights waiting on the product designer's weekly progress reports. We would usually talk about twice a week. The designer juggled a full-time job, a hobby of building his own experimental airplanes, and building a Radio Fence receiver. So the updates were not always as fulfilling as I had hoped. In late spring of 1991, I impatiently called asking how close we were getting to the planned launch, for word had gotten out, and pressure was beginning to build to introduce a product. I anxiously called on Sunday evening hopeful of great progress over the weekend. Unfortunately, the designer informed me his grass had gotten really high, and he had to spend the weekend mowing it (he lived on a large tract)! Such are the perils of contract engineering. During that time I dreamed of how great it must be to have a full-time engineering staff of my very own!

In spite of all that, we had a design that seemed to meet our specifications by May of 1991. In June we were ready to go into production. The plan was to contract with Fi-Shock to do the assembly. Since they didn't have surface mount equipment, the initial products, both transmitter and receiver, were a through-hole design. There were no microprocessors, but then Invisible Fence didn't have any either.

DIY KITS SOLD BY RETAILERS WILL NEVER WORK

As with any new idea or venture, there are many more naysayers than cheerleaders, and Radio Fence was no exception. One of the first people I showed our prototypes to was the Invisible Fence dealer in Knoxville who had been so helpful. At first he was surprised and shocked that we had developed a competitive product. However, as I demonstrated our product and described our business plan, he became more incredulous and reassured. Radio Fence was going to pioneer a new way of marketing pet containment systems by creating a "starter kit" in an eye-catching package that would be sold to consumers through retail outlets. We supplied installation and training by including a video and training booklet in the kit, and for after-purchase service, we would supply a toll-free number.

The dealer was polite but very critical. For fifteen years, the Invisible Fence Company had only sold their product as a professionally-installed system with additional training support and local on-site trouble-shooting provided by the local dealer. The dealer could relate a series of service-nightmare stories. He would be called in the middle of the night or on weekends by customers demanding he come to their house immediately to change a battery or fix a wire. "This is a service business," he confidently pointed out, "and self-service kits will never work."

WHY LITTLE THINGS ARE SO IMPORTANT

We assume that things in our everyday lives have some divine logic, but often they are in fact, just the result of random chance, necessity, or convenience somewhere back in history. At Radio Systems there are many examples of our attention to little things. We believe in "try a lot of things and keep what works," which means most things that we do today were at one time just an experiment or test that went well.

A good example is why we sell 500' rolls of wire. I remember once visiting a potential customer who was comparing our products to one of our competitors, and he cited the competitor as saying that the reason why wire came in 500' spools was because extensive research had shown that it was the appropriate length for the average consumer. This competitor was one of our knock-off competitors from China and had absolutely no historical data of its own. They assumed in their copying of our products that because we used 500' of wire and that since we had 95% market share at the time, then we must have had a research-driven reason for our choice.

Invisible Fence only sold 1,000' rolls of wire, and our data collected from our warranty cards showed that the average customer used 1,100' of wire. However, we were the first company back in 1991 to sell wire in 500' rolls. Why? The reason was simple convenience. Saco sold electric fence wire on spools that held ¼ mile of bare stainless steel 17-gauge wire. We had selected 18-gauge, insulated wire as Radio Fence's antennae cable. The only spools we had to wind it on were the electric fence wire spools. When wound on this spool, you guessed it, it held right at 500' of the insulated wire. We considered finding a different spool that would hold 1,000' of wire, but there were several problems. First, it would raise the cost of our kit significantly.

Second, and most importantly, it wouldn't fit in the box we had. Thus, with divine insight and exhaustive research, 500' was established as the length of choice. It was with some delight that I heard competition referring to this length as providential!

Why 18-gauge? First and importantly, our electronic design was such that we could use thinner gauge wire than Invisible Fence. By generating a sine wave rather than a square wave, we could use very thin wire. However, we needed to make sure the wire wouldn't break while being installed, so we couldn't make it too thin. Why not 17 or 19 or 22-gauge? Fi-Shock had barrels of 18-gauge, multi-stranded, copper-tinned wire, and our engineer said that would work fine for our product tests. In the tests the wire was easy to work with. Our electronic components provider said he could give us a deal on it by combining our purchases with Fi-Shock. Thus, 18-gauge became the standard for the company's first ten years.

THE RADIO FENCE CORPORATION

The first product, Radio Fence, was named before the company was named, indicative of how products and product development drove our early strategy and still does to this day. The Invisible Fence company had a product by the same name. After working with the designer on the first product design, I became familiar with radio-frequency technology and maybe being too close to the science of it, thought that "Radio Fence" was appropriate. Besides, I knew we'd sell the product no matter what the name.

Sometime in the spring of 1991, the need to set up a separate checking account for the company that was to own the Radio Fence product became apparent, so I drove to the bank and sat at the branch officer's desk. She asked an obvious question, "What name do you want the account to be under?" I paused. Just like the naming of Saco, I had never given any thought to naming this new company! The first thought was just putting the name of the product on the account, but that didn't seem appropriate. So I just added the word "corporation" to the end, and we had our first corporate name, *Radio Fence Corporation.*

I hear stories of companies starting with millions of dollars in seed capital from venture capitalists and how they burn through it in just a few years. We didn't have that worry. We had no seed capital from venture capitalists or anyone for that matter. Saco paid the bills Radio Fence had, primarily the engineering invoices. When it came time to go into production,

I got several vendors of Saco to stand as credit references and managed to buy what we needed on credit. Then we would require cash in advance (sometimes way, way, way in advance!) from our customers. Amazingly, we survived this way for close to a year before we progressed to factoring receivables. It wasn't until late 1993, two and a half years after we started, that we took in the first outside capital. During this time I maintained 100% ownership, and of course, 100% of the liabilities.

In June of 1991, many good things happened. I had hoped to sell 100 units per month and expected most of that to be sold through Saco. Instead we sold 3,000 Radio Fence products in the first month. Orders for 2,000 units came from new, installing dealers.

My father, Tom Boyd, made a sales call on Home Quarters (HQ), a small start-up home center located in Virginia Beach with about thirty stores at the time. He was there selling his products, but at the end of the presentation, he brought out a sample Radio Fence. The buyer had absolutely no interest. As he was getting ready to leave, Dad asked if an old friend, Mike Pastore, who was the president of Home Quarters and had known Dad for some time, was in.

Note by Tom Boyd: A few years earlier I had taken members of Mike Pastore's team on a trip as my guests to a pro-celebrity tennis event in Nevis-St. Kitts. They spent the week with movie stars Lloyd Bridges, Dick Van Patten, and several others.

The buyer called his boss, and he came in to say hello. When he saw the Radio Fence sample on the table, he got very excited. "I always wanted to start my own business and compete with Invisible Fence myself!" he exclaimed. He looked to the buyer and said, "We are putting these in aren't we?" "Of course," the buyer told his boss. With that bit of luck, we were on our way.

The next day we had orders for a dozen Radio Fence systems per store or around 500 units. It was our first major order. HQ was recognized as a pioneer and industry leader, and others watched them closely. The fact that they had added the product was a very useful reference over the next few years.

There were a few other notable accounts that got us started. One was Damark. In August of 1991, our rep agency in Minneapolis called and wanted to know if we would sell to Damark, a mail order catalog company. They would buy 50 Radio Fence kits at the going cost of $250 each and offer them in their October catalog. But there was a catch - they would have to be on consignment, and they would only pay for what they sold. Again this might sound like an easy decision in retrospect. However, at the time, we were backordering everyone by an average of three months. Some of those customers had paid in advance and were beginning to suspect a scam (more on this later), and we still had no cash in spite of our pay-in-advance terms. So I had to balance the fact that we couldn't ship with the possibility of some free advertising (I wasn't very optimistic they would actually sell our product). We decided to take a chance, and it turned out to be fortuitous. The Radio Fence was an amazing success for them, and they were one of our top three accounts for the next five years. For Damark, Radio Fence was one of their best-selling products. In spite of the fact that we were always on the top of their weekly backorder report, we had a great partnership. In addition to their significant purchases, their catalogs did generate a lot of publicity and awareness that we could not otherwise have afforded to buy.

For everything positive that happened in June, July had an equal amount of negative. We soon found that we just couldn't produce the product as designed. When it was produced, it had a 100% fail rate in the field after at most one week, and we were already getting vendors pressing for payment. At the same time all this hit, I got a certified letter from Invisible Fence about five pages long accusing me of all sorts of mean and despicable crimes for having used the word "invisible" in our description of the product.

We had decided to call our system "Radio Fence, the invisible pet containment system." Being a novice to the legal world, it was a very unnerving and threatening letter. I realize now that it was just a lot of bluster. However, at the time, it worked. Our attorney and their attorneys agreed to cease and desist, and we signed an agreement that we would never use the word "invisible" in any of our communications again.

By July of 1991, Howard Fehl and two others had joined Radio Fence Corporation, and there wasn't room for all of us in Saco's trailer any longer, so we leased what we referred to as a "modular office" and had it installed in a small lot behind Fi-Shock. In fact, it was what's better known in the mobile home community as a doublewide and had been used by a dealer as an office. It was always a challenge recruiting new employees when they drove up to a doublewide sitting in a back lot of another company's factory. In spite of this, we were lucky to gather a great team.

THE PIONEERS

As I have previously stated, a bit of brilliant inspiration supported by hard work and a lot of great people can take you a long, long way. The pioneers are the great people who were there at the beginning of Radio Fence Corporation. Their dedication and contributions built the firm foundation that is today's Radio Systems. While I have refrained from using actual names throughout these writings, the pioneers need to be recognized.

Though I hate to admit it (explanation later), one of the most important figures in our early history was Stuart Stallings. In fact, Stuart became an employee of Radio Fence several months before me, and it was his success that convinced me to change my official employment and give my full attention to this new company.

Stuart was a childhood friend I had lost contact with after high school. One day in 1990, he showed up at the trailer selling printing supplies. The printing business was tough, and he was looking to do something new. He started working for Saco in the fall of 1990 and switched to the Radio Fence Company in May of 1991, making him our first full-time employee. Having no employees and no sales, I freely bestowed the title of vice president – sales.

There was tremendous, pent-up demand for our products by individuals who had seen the success of Invisible Fence dealers and wanted to start a competing franchise. Stuart was great at finding these potential dealers. To get started with us, they were required to sign an "Authorized Sales and Installation Center" (ASIC) agreement. They were required to buy a minimum of twenty units at $250 each. If they bought 50 or a 100 units, they could get a bigger territory. There was always great demand for every territory, Stuart assured them, but they could lock it up by signing the agreement and sending in their check. Stuart's goal was at least 20 units or one ASIC per day, a goal he regularly achieved. That $5,000 prepayment was the key to our cash flow. Stuart had a great personality and was very creative. In fact, he created the original Radio Fence logo with the dog in the middle. His objective was to give the product a softer, established, more comfortable look, so that consumers would not feel as intimidated by the technology. He told me he got the idea from a trucking company's logo he saw on the back of a truck one day.

Our second employee was Melanie Thomas. She had been Saco's office manager for about one year prior to my starting Radio Fence. She had a good second-in-command at Saco in Teresa Leek. As the Radio Fence business started taking up more and more time in July of 1991, she started taking half her pay from each company. By year-end, she was a full time Radio Fence employee.

Melanie was an amazing lady, totally dedicated and with an unbelievable capacity for work. She never left before 7:00 p.m., usually worked until 9:00 or 10:00, and often would work around the clock. When we talk about the sweat equity that built the company, a major part of it was hers. It was a great loss when she left us in late 1993, and there were many among us who wondered if we could survive without her. In fact, I got an anonymous letter stating that we were doomed without her, and I had to do something to get her back. Unfortunately she had difficult family problems that took precedence and required her to relocate back to Utah.

Our third full-time employee was Howard Fehl. I still remember the first time I met Howard (who doesn't?). In July we were desperate for engineering help. Our product wasn't working, and our contract engineer was only part-time and not available to commit the time necessary to help us resolve our daily crises. A new circuit board vendor recommended an engineer out of Bristol, Tennessee, who had recently left Raytheon Corporation. I called Howard, and he said he was interested, and we agreed to an interview in Knoxville that included sitting in on a trouble-shooting meeting.

Howard had a degree from DeVry Technical College in Chicago where he grew up. He had traveled around the country working for several major high-tech companies, including over ten years at General Dynamics in California. He was a family man, a big family man! He had six children and a few grandchildren, many of whom were still living with him at home.

Howard met me briefly in my Dad's office at Fi-Shock (there was no space in the trailer), and then we went into a meeting with a manufacturing consultant, Bill Franklin, the designer, Stuart Stallings, and my father as an observer. I was a young-looking, late-forties guy with long, blond, curly-permed hair and glasses. He sat in the back of the room and didn't comment during the discussions but smiled and nodded knowingly throughout every topic as if he had seen it all before and had the easy answers. Afterwards he confidently asserted he could help and was hired on a three-month trial basis.

I was concerned about him needing to relocate from Bristol, but he convinced me that driving ninety miles a day to work each way was no big deal, that working in Chicago and Los Angeles had conditioned him to long commutes. He managed this commute for almost two years before finally moving a little closer to Morristown, only 15 miles away.

I soon discovered that Howard wasn't quite the board-level designer I had thought. However, I believe I got much more than I expected. Howard was then, as he is now, a tireless worker. He took over key aspects of purchasing, all technical calls from consumers, and product development, which primarily consisted of working with the design engineer at our circuit board vendor. He was today's equivalent of VP-global sourcing, director of consumer service, and VP-product development all rolled into one. And, as everyone had to be, he was flexible. He would work out of Fi-Shock's cafeteria part of the day because we had no desk for him nor any room for one. When he needed to use the phone, he would walk down to the trailer looking for one not being used, then ask the person if he could use it, calling from over their shoulder as they worked.

While I consider myself somewhat demanding (in fairness, with myself, too), Howard made even me cringe. A supplier would be in his office (a few years later, when he had an office), and I would know that we hadn't paid this supplier in months and felt very beholden to them. I would step in and find Howard berating them, demanding better pricing, better delivery, and better terms. I always felt sorry for my fellow peddler and left in awe of Howard's pluckiness. Howard went from being our entire engineering and operations department to in charge of all procurement to, years later, vice president of development and then to Liaison for all Asian sourcing. Without exception he had shown himself a flexible, loyal, tireless, and tenacious member of our team.

Other key members of the original staff were Christy Phillips (who did general clerical duties and whose mother worked next door at Fi-Shock), Chuck Ferrell and Darrell McCroskey (our two electrical technicians direct from the Air Force), Brenda (who took over consumer and dealer calls in August), a receptionist, and Stuart Stallings, our VP-sales. It was a small but close-knit team that rose to the many challenges, and believe me, there were plenty of them.

MANY CHALLENGES

When I give the 30-minute version of company history, strategy, and vision for the future, all of about one minute is spent on the first few years and is glossed over with a statement something like "In that first six months, we reached one million in sales, $5 million the next year, and have achieved 50% compound growth since." There's usually a spiffy graph highlighting this. I still think to myself about the irony of this presentation every time I give it. It is presented as if we did not have a care in the world. The truth is, every day was a struggle for survival. I would come home so stressed I couldn't eat or sleep. One night in the spring of 1992, my wife, Jenny, implored me to quit it all and just go back to selling electric fencing. But there was no way I could. In part, I still held on to a dream of what could be. In part, I was committed to all the people – customers, employees, and vendors who counted on me.

But mostly, I could not see any way out. I was too busy trying to construct a way to survive another day to find a way to escape. At this point you might wonder what could be so bad. It's hard to isolate just a few things, but I'll try. First, there was the product – it didn't work, and customers' beloved pets paid the price when it didn't. Receivers leaked, transformers shorted out, parts lost contact on the board, and hundreds of everyday things such as garage door openers, televisions, and thunder would cause them to falsely shock the dog. I should mention here that while uncomfortable, dogs were not permanently injured. Second, there was the cash flow; there wasn't any. We had no financing and survived only by getting customers to pay in advance and by delaying payments to vendors months after their due dates (we didn't establish a real bank relationship until 1994). Third, we had supply chain issues – we couldn't ship. We could only ship on average 10% of an order, and most were months late. In sum, we had customers screaming for their shipments, and then when they got shipped, they were screaming about the quality. There was a lot of screaming.

TECHNICAL PROBLEMS

To those of you less technically minded, I hope my discussion of these problems doesn't bore you. But the bulk of our current products' design and function has its origin in our early history, much of which you might take for granted. Its relevance should make it interesting, and hopefully there is a lesson or two that you can derive from it.

A first lesson – Don't assume the competition knows what they are doing! This is a lesson I learned early, and unfortunately, have repeated too often. When the designer created the original design, he made the assumption that the Invisible Fence receiver design was fundamentally sound and basically set out to make an improvement or two. All too often, we make the assumption that because another successful company is doing something a certain way, then it must be an acceptable way. In reality, for all we know, that company is having a crisis as a result of their decisions, or they simply don't know how to do it better.

We did make several innovations. First, we designed the first sine wave transmitter. Invisible Fence sent out a square wave, which in layman's terms meant it sent out just a lot of noise. Thus any noise on their broadcast frequency, that being 10.65 KHz, would cause their receiver to false shock the dog. Thunder, televisions, and other low noise could register at this frequency, falsely activating the receiver. With the sine wave, we broadcast a cleaner and more efficient signal. We could send our signal through a much thinner wire a much greater distance. Where Invisible Fence had to use 14-gauge wire to carry their signal 1,000 feet, we could send a signal many times that on just 18-gauge wire. For Invisible Fence to send the signal further, their installers sold a $400 power booster and used a heavier, more expensive 12-gauge wire.

While we trumped them on distance, we didn't fare as well on false signals. We assumed we were no worse than they were so that must be OK, right? Wrong. They, too, were having tremendous difficulties with false activations. However, they had local installers available to visit the customer in the middle of the night and console them or try to advise them on how to avoid a problem. With our do-it-yourself system, we did not have that luxury. When a false activation occurred, the consumer was justifiably very upset. They would call and scream at whomever they could get on the phone at Radio Systems (we had no call center back then) and then return the product for a refund.

Sometimes we could figure out what was causing the false activations, but most often we couldn't. I recall one consumer who called and reached me (a one-in-six chance as everyone, all six of us, were responsible for picking up the ringing line). He had bought the system three months prior with no problems. Then one day he came home from work and found his dog shivering on the back porch. He listened and heard the sound of the receiver activating every couple of seconds. His dog had been getting continuous shocks for most of the day! This wasn't your average irate customer; he was livid.

We struggled with screening out false signals for several years, going through many generations of code. It took the introduction of the VLSI ASIC chip (more on that later) to finally solve the problem. Also, as I will relate later, this was the single biggest reason for so many of our imitators going out of business in the years to follow.

Originally, we used a through-hole design of the receiver board assuming that Fi-Shock, who could only do through-hole, would be our OEM supplier. Unfortunately, the design was too meticulous for them. There were days in which four women would spend an eight-hour shift, make 100 boards, have 70% fail initial inspection, and only a dozen made it through final assembly.

Through another contact of Bill Franklin, we sent the PCBA fabrication to a company in Asheville, North Carolina, SDX. SDX had an engineer who recommended that we change to a surface mount design on the receiver and also that we add a microprocessor.

At a nominal cost, I think less than $5,000, he redesigned the receiver to these specifications, all in about 60 days time. As a result in November of 1991, we were the first company in the pet containment industry to introduce a microprocessor-based system, one of our many innovation "firsts."

We also had a small problem with the batteries; they would explode on occasion! At the time we were using a stack of five 1.5-volt button cells that were tacked together and then shrink-wrapped. Contracting to have these custom batteries made for us was an adventure in itself. If the consumer put the battery in backwards, they would heat up and explode. We quickly developed a new design that included a diode that gave us reverse polarity protection. The batteries were expensive, $15 at retail, and would only last a few months at best, but at least they didn't detonate.

PRODUCTION PROBLEMS

Since 1993, Radio Systems has progressively had more and more of our products assembled and packaged in other countries, mostly China. On occasion when there is either a quality or production issue, I'll overhear someone complain about the situation and reduce the issue to the fact that the supplier is in another country. While this is convenient, my experience leads me to believe it is far too simplistic. Good suppliers and bad suppliers are all over the world, and production issues don't magically go away just because your manufacturing is in the next room or within a day's drive.

Our two primary circuit board suppliers were SDX in Asheville, who made receiver boards, and Incor in Soddy-Daisy, Tennessee, who made transmitter boards. For two years running, we averaged less than 50% of requested shipments being delivered on time. Of those shipments, incoming inspections would yield usually a 40% failure rate. Unfortunately, our volume was too small to attract many large OEM PCBA suppliers. Somewhere during this time I heard the axiom "You can't test in quality; it has to be designed in," and it was true that most of our difficulties were a result of the designs themselves. This is a truth that has proven itself many times over in our history.

During 1991 and the first half of 1992, Fi-Shock did our final assembly. However, by the summer of 1992, Bill Franklin again recommended I hire a manufacturing expert to review our processes. He suggested I visit with Larry Manning, who was available as a consultant after his last company, Visicon, went out of business.

Larry took the consulting job and quickly convinced me that we needed him full-time as an operations manager. The fact that his official office was to be the break room in our doublewide (excuse me, our "modular office") with no plans for much more did not deter him. Larry was one of the key leaders in our first five years and personally brought in many of today's key associates including Steve Baker, Phil Green, Bill Groh, and Walt Frankewich.

Larry and I came to the conclusion that we could save lots of money by taking over our own final assembly. There was a vacant 1950s-style building down the street that was formerly owned by TRW. The roof leaked, the ventilation was poor, and it had only one loading dock. But to us, it was the Taj Mahal. We moved the warehousing and assembly operation there in May of 1992, and the rest of the company followed in August of that year.

Taking over manufacturing was no nirvana. During the years that we did our own final assembly, we consistently had an unacceptable scrap cost due to manufacturing inefficiencies of 5% or more. In 1992, this resulted in over a half-million dollars in scrapped product. This problem was due to either shorting the circuit boards during the assembly process, bad potting, or a dozen other possibilities. The bottom line was that we weren't very good at manufacturing.

One of the lower points in our delivery problems was the day I made a customer cry. Stuart Stallings had set the customer up as one of our first ASICs in the fall of 1991. She had been forewarned that there were going to be shipping problems when Stuart showed up for her first home show with none of the product she had prepaid for, and he had promised to bring to the show with him. Not to be stopped, they solved the problem brilliantly. They filled the booth with empty boxes Stuart had brought with him to display and put large, bright "Sold" stickers on each. They still had no product, but they gave the impression to passers-by that this was a product in demand!

In the spring of 1992, we were still back-ordering everyone, including the same customer (the original order had been shipped, though). She called one morning distraught over our lack of shipment. She had consumers yelling at her demanding delivery of their fence, and she was very frustrated and upset. After I explained to her that I wasn't going to be able to ship to her again that week, she broke down and started crying. I had been cursed at, threatened with lawsuits, and even with strangulation, but hadn't made anyone cry (to my knowledge). We were over-allocated, but I did manage to find units for her that week. She has since grown her business incredibly. By 2001, she is one of Radio Systems' top ten customers, distributing to over 300 other dealers and through the Internet. And she hasn't had to cry since.

RISING TO THE CHALLENGES

Next I want to tell you about the Pillow Club. In our first year, as you might imagine, we had huge challenges and extremely limited resources. The result – we all worked incredibly long hours. There were several who made a habit of putting in a 24-hour shift, literally working around the clock and then some. Our office manager probably put in the most of these marathon sessions. However, other team members and myself, not wanting to be outdone when it came to martyrdom, put in a few as well. So we created the Pillow Club, and to belong, one had to put in a 24-hour shift. We discussed having a trophy of some sort consisting of a decorated pillow, but we never seemed to have time to follow through on it. Though there were tremendous demands on everyone, all believed in our future.

By our first Thanksgiving, we had a dedicated team. The night before Thanksgiving, 1991, will always be one to remember. One of our dealers from Nashville, who was desperate for product, and I worked all night. Our receptionist and Stuart worked until around 9:00 p.m. waiting for another team member to return from our board supplier in North Carolina with PCBAs for the RF201 receiver. They promised 200 but they only managed to supply us with around 80.

When they arrived, we immediately set up a makeshift assembly line along our conference table (a folding table in my office). At the time, Fi-Shock was our contract manufacturer for final assembly, but they were closed until the following Monday, and we had to have product right then because our Nashville dealer had upset, screaming customers demanding replacements. One thing we lacked was a proper tester to check the shock level. Our customer had received many complaints that the product shock level wasn't sufficient, and he didn't trust our electronic testers. To her great credit, our receptionist volunteered for the last position on the assembly line, which consisted of inserting the battery, placing the receiver next to the short-loop wire hooked to the transmitter, activating the receiver, and then grabbing hold! Fortunately for her, about 40 of the 80 were defective or had insufficient shock. By midnight, we had 40 units produced. Our customer left with his product, a confidence in the shock level, and an appreciation for our dedication.

Going Greyhound. When all is dead throughout Knoxville around 4:00 a.m., one only needs to go to the Greyhound bus station to find the action. You go Greyhound when FedEx is just too darn slow. Using the Next Bus Out service, our supplier in Asheville could take their day's production to their Greyhound terminal around 10:00 p.m. in the evening, and it would arrive in Knoxville at around 4:00 a.m. This timing was absolutely necessary, as we had to conformal-coat the boards, a process that took at least two hours before we could use them. Thus, someone would have to get the boards at 4:00 a.m., take them to the factory (Fi-Shock's the first year, ours the second), hang them on a clothes-line-type rack, and spray them with conformal coating, so that by 7:00 a.m. when it was time for production to start, they would be dry.

While we had a great team, I didn't have the heart to delegate this duty to anyone else. Besides, it was on my way into work. So I became a regular at Greyhound, truly; it's the happening place in the wee hours of the morning. Not only was it busy, but you could also see the most interesting people.

There were a few occasions that we couldn't even wait for Greyhound. Several times we talked our supplier into running a second shift until past midnight, which meant they would miss the bus. So I would drive over to their factory and wait for them to package up the circuit boards, then drive them back to Knoxville for the next morning's assembly.

Regardless of what our vendor promised us the afternoon before, every morning was a mystery full of hope and dread. Invariably we would have demand for three to four thousand systems for the week but were only able to get commitments for half that many boards. So we would plan our ship schedule (sworn promises to the customers) based on this. We would average getting 75% of what our vendors committed to, and then, on an average week, half those would fail in production. Thus, our usual week would start with a demand of 4,000 Radio Fences. Monday mornings I would call all our customers and promise their portion of the 2,000 I thought I was going to be able to build based on promises from my vendors. By the weekend, some components invariably didn't ship, and about 40% of the product failed going down the assembly line. Thus we would ship only 800 to 1,000 units. Waking up and going to the bus stop was not a problem; I was wide awake with anticipation (or dread) anyway!

CASH FLOW OR LACK THEREOF

Many companies get started by "bootstrapping." I've never read the definition of that term, but I believe we were at least an order of magnitude less well-financed! Though we did manage to pay the initial debt of $26,000 back to Saco in 1991, we struggled.

As mentioned earlier, a substantial amount of our early cash flow came from potential dealers putting down their deposits for product weeks and even months before shipment. Another substantial group of unwitting lenders were our suppliers. Selling product was not very difficult at the time. Most of my sales efforts went to selling suppliers to make that next shipment! However, these tactics were not enough to finance a fast-growing business, especially with the growth of sales to conventional retailers such as Home Quarters, Agway, and Damark who required terms, so we had to explore other alternatives.

We had no outside investors with myself owning 100% of the company. Even though my friend, Todd Birdwell, was Saco's banker at First Tennessee, since Radio Fence Corporation had no history and no assets, our bank wouldn't consider us for financial help. Todd and I still talk about the ski vacation we took in the winter of 1992 where I would have to go to a pay phone after every other run and try to talk a vendor not only out of suing us, but in making the next shipment.

Fi-Shock's former CFO had left my father's company in 1985 and went to work for the Resolution Trust Company leading a team to restructure or liquidate the numerous, failing savings and loans around the country at that time. He had started his own factoring business exclusively doing so for Fi-Shock. By the fall of 1991, we had arranged for him to factor our major accounts.

For those not familiar with factoring, it is somewhere just above loan sharking and the pawnshop business. First one "sells" the invoice to the factoring company for a discount, in our case 5%. Thus, the customer would send the check to the factoring company rather than the manufacturer. The factoring company would advance 75% of the 95% on the day of the invoice. If the customer was late in payment, the money was deducted from future advances. Simultaneously, interest is paid on the advance. In our case, this was at an annual rate of 18%. In addition, I would pledge everything the company and I personally owned as collateral, including my home (something that hasn't changed to this day). All told, we were paying a very high cost of capital.

There is an adage that one should not begrudge what the other person makes in a transaction but only be concerned with what you earn. This was the only justifiable way to look at our financing costs in those days. Though we paid exorbitant rates, we felt fortunate to get any financing at all. It was due to companies such as Pack Enterprises and their successor in 1993, a factoring company from Dallas whose name I can't recall, that we survived and eventually prospered. Some margin is always better than no margin.

ENOUGH THINGS RIGHT TO CARRY US THROUGH

By reading all our trials and tribulations, one might get the impression that there was no reason to even be in business. I must confess that there is a degree of posturing to address those who are tempted one day to say, "Gee, they sure were lucky" and imagine our start as a walk in the park. Also, I still cringe when I hear someone make a comment about the "good old days" or how much more difficult things are today than when we got started. After surviving those "good old days," I felt that I and all those that endured them would be prepared for anything the future would hold.

However, we did have a lot of good fortune and many great successes in those early days. When I created Radio Fence, I had hoped for a product that I could sell 100 units each month. I assumed Saco would be the primary customer probably buying 90% of the product. In fact, Radio Fence turned out not to be a great product for Saco customers at that time, and they accounted for very little of the sales in the first half-dozen years.

The original cost of the kit was around $60 to manufacture, and we sold it for $250. This may have been the best margin in our history for any product. Thus, even at a mere 100 units a month, I assumed we could clear about $15,000 per month. Considering it had taken me seven years to save $26,000 with Saco, this seemed like pretty heady stuff.

We started taking orders in mid-May of 1991, and by the time we started shipping the first of June, we already had a backlog of 500 units. Then we got the Home Quarters account and had an additional 800 units to ship. Another dealer in New York committed to 1,000 units. By the end of June, we had a backlog of 3,000 units for immediate shipment! I'll spare you the math, but as you might imagine, we were excited. Yes, there were major hurdles ahead in quality, supply, and finance, but as long as there was this kind of demand and these margins, we had the most important ingredients needed to succeed.

In 1991, we ended the year with a profit of approximately $30,000 ($55,200/2018). Considering all the problems, we were elated. If we could just get a few things right, we reasoned, we would have a very profitable business.

The installing dealer base, our ASICs, was important and accounted for 45% of our sales for the year. On the strength of Home Quarters alone, the home center market represented 34%. The balance of 21% went through mail order, primarily Damark.

In 1992, demand was increasing at a geometric rate. Our sales that year increased by 500%, from $980,000 ($1.7 million/2018) to $4.9 million ($8.7 million/2018), over three times the sales of Saco. More and more dealers wanted to get involved in the business. It was a very flattering experience; individuals were calling up to tell us they would quit their jobs and commit what would be a significant investment for them to be a dealer, our "ASIC." I had people like a product before but never so much that they were willing to quit their jobs to be part of it.

Our most significant growth came from retailers. In 1992, Agway began buying in earnest. They had a very good buyer who helped us to grow the business at Agway, but he also had little sympathy for backorders. I very clearly remember sitting at my desk in the modular office in the spring of 1992 contemplating how I was going to call that day's customers and explain yet again that we weren't going to make our promises. Earlier that day I had talked to our sales representative for Agway, and she commented that of all the problems to have, having too much demand is one of the best ones. Since I had nothing better to offer, I thought I would use that one on the Agway buyer. When I did, there was complete silence on the other end of the phone. Then with a noticeably restrained, steady but intent voice, he slowly said, "If I could jump through this phone right now and put my hands around your neck and strangle you, I would!" Don't think less of him. I spent my days having the same conversation with all of our customers; he was just much more eloquent than most. Interestingly, he later became a salesman for Radio Systems.

Other major new customers were Tractor Supply, Ace, Cotter (now TruServ), Wolverton (a distributor who serviced Quality Stores), Pet Supplies Plus, and Ames. We were going to these retailers with no brand name, a brand new product, and since we raised the price in 1992 from $250 to $275, a very expensive product that would have to retail for $399 to $499. Outside of consumer electronics or power equipment, such retails were very rare. For a pet item, it was beyond consideration. For that reason, most of our success came with the farm and hardware/home center trade. In fact, after Pet Supplies Plus, we didn't sell another major pet chain until 1995.

For those in sales, you will recognize that such a proposition would be a difficult sell, so we sold everything on a guaranteed sale. There is no way retailers would take the risk themselves. We figured it was better to find out sooner rather than later if our product would succeed at retail. We also offered aggressive co-op advertising. If they would put us in a circular, we would pay for 100% of the cost of an ad, and we aggressively lobbied for these since this was our only form of advertising. And, of course, having a few success stories such as HQ, Damark, and Agway to build on was key.

Sales by channel for 1992 were 33% mail order with Damark becoming our number one customer, followed by home centers at 25%. Independent dealers dropped to 24% of the total though our sales to them doubled. Ames, who did a small test in October of 1992, gave us 2% of our total sales to mass merchants.

However, Radio Fence was not the only company having success. Everyone in the industry was doing well. All the new companies were having great success, and Invisible Fence was also increasing sales. While sales growth is great, if it comes merely as a result of gaining market share within a stagnate category, the future is limited. In our case, we were part of an exploding industry. Of course, no one really enjoys seeing their competitors prosper, but we were consoled with the fact that we were the fastest growing of the bunch and finished the year second only to Invisible Fence in revenues.

MARKETING INNOVATIONS

If we can take credit for one major innovation in these early years, it was in pioneering a new marketing approach. Invisible Fence sold through franchise dealers who sold direct to the public. Every other company entering the business in 1991, and there were many (Dog Guard, DogWatch, Freedom Fence, and Innotek, to name a few), all copied the Invisible Fence marketing strategy of setting up franchise-installing dealers. While Radio Fence did set up dealers, it was only a part of our marketing strategy.

Radio Fence was the first to put the product in a do-it-yourself package that included a lithograph box designed for retailers. We were the first to include a video in every package. We were also the first to add a toll-free number, so the consumer could call one central hotline for service, a necessity since we were selling through retailers.

I'd like to take credit for this innovation by saying it was a brilliant, breakthrough insight. The truth of the matter was that selling to retailers was all I knew. I knew nothing about the franchise dealer business. As late as 1994, I ran into our Dog Watch competitor at the American Pet Products Manufacturers Association show and was told that he was just waiting for the pet containment business through retailers to collapse and that he was still convinced it wouldn't work. I think it's safe to say today that he was wrong.

Drawing from my Saco experience with electric fencing, we introduced the first lifetime warranty that included damage by lightning. Saco's principal selling proposition was its service. We offered a lifetime warranty that included lightning, a major issue with electric fencing. The competition forced their consumers to send their product back to the factory, and repairs could run half the cost of the unit and take weeks. Saco had fence energizers that could be opened up by the dealer and circuit boards that could be replaced in minutes. New boards were $19.65, but we would trade out an old, damaged board with a replacement for only $6.00 to cover labor. It was this experience that led us to offering a similar warranty at Radio Systems, and we still do today.

By offering the lifetime warranty, we had a far superior warranty than our competition, and many customers bought our product initially because of it and then stuck with us as a result of it. Although there were many problems satisfying the customer, we never gave up trying and would continue to replace or repair as long as the customer was willing to work with us. We learned that if we stood by our product, even when it wasn't perfect, our customers would stand by us.

In 1992, we had aspirations of one day selling to Sears. We were, in fact, going to be listed in the Sears catalog in 1993 (they planned a long way out; unfortunately ours was the catalog scheduled to be printed right before they closed the catalog operation). In order to sell Sears, any electrical product had to be listed by Underwriter's Laboratories. Having grown up with electric fencing, where getting a UL listing was critical, getting a UL listing for Radio Fence was something I had been anticipating.

I personally took on the project of getting the Radio Fence listing, and it was quite a learning experience. Underwriter's Laboratories' primary focus was on fire safety, not electrical safety or efficacy. It turned out that UL was an independent company with no government requirements to set standards for products. Since ours was a new category, there was no standard in place. To create a standard, it was strictly an economic proposition for them – would enough companies get in the market and apply for a UL listing to justify them going to the expense of creating a standard? Further, they were concerned with liability – they didn't want the UL listing to imply that the Radio Fence system would keep the dog in.

In order to get them to set a standard, a meeting was arranged at their offices in Chicago where I presented our case to several vice presidents, the head of engineering, a project engineer, and a couple of their legal advisors. The meeting lasted over three hours. In the end, they were convinced that this was a new business in which they wanted to be involved. They had two standards – a listing and a classification. A listing implied that the product was electrically safe and would not cause harm to people or animals. A classification implied that the product would perform as advertised. They were still unconvinced that they could assure a consumer that it would work every time to keep the dog in the yard, so they agreed to offer listings.

Since there was no standard to apply for, we had to help them write one. This process took nearly a year to do and cost us three to four times what anyone else would subsequently have to pay. However, we were the first to get a UL listing and could make the claim that we not only met the standard, we set it! Being the only UL listed pet containment system was another key feature that set us apart.

Last, there is always price. Of our competitors, we were the least expensive even at $250 in 1991 and $275 in 1992. Invisible Fence was the most expensive, with an uninstalled kit retailing for around $850, and the rest of the competitors fell somewhere in between.

TECHNOLOGICAL INNOVATIONS

While we had major quality and production issues with our design, it did have some very innovative aspects. As already discussed, by using a sine wave, we had the strongest transmitter in the industry and could enclose bigger yards for less money than any of the competition.

In November of 1991, as mentioned, we were the first to introduce a microprocessor-based system. This gave us many advantages. We were the first to send out two signals, one that gave the dog a warning at one point and then about 20% closer in, a correction. No other company had this feature. Invisible Fence had a single signal and one-second delay from warning to shock. Thus, a fast running dog could be through a barrier before it got its first correction. This feature that we called "warning based on distance" was a big selling feature. It's still an advantage we have over most of our contemporary competitors; we've just added so many newer, competitive advantages that we sometimes get bored with some of the older ones and fail to emphasize them.

Another big feature was that the microprocessor provided us with better screening of false signals. It wasn't perfect, but it was equal to or better than anything else on the market and a quantum leap forward from what we had before. While we still got complaints, the worst was over.

One of our greatest virtues then and today is our commitment to continuous improvement. Unlike the competition, who could solve problems by sending a local franchisee to the consumer's home, we were forced to add as many features as possible to the product to overcome problems. We had to be better out of necessity.

One of the best contributions came not from an engineer but from a couple of our technicians, Darrell McCroskey and Chuck Ferrell. One of our biggest complaints from consumers was that they were not getting enough range. Invariably, they would send the transmitter in, and it would work just fine. They simply had a poor installation. Invisible Fence could go and troubleshoot the wire. Without that luxury, we had to compensate with a product. In order to do this, we added a "high/low" switch on our transmitter. In low, the transmitter would be sufficient for nearly any size yard, up to 25 acres. However, if the customer had a bad installation, the range could be less than a foot. When switched to the high mode, the range would jump back to an acceptable 10' or so. This innovation was a basic feature of our deluxe pet containment transmitters for 10 years.

In 1992, Larry Manning also hired Joe Babb, Radio Systems' first design engineer. Formerly of Visicon, Joe was a bluegrass singer with a beard who preferred overalls or jeans. And he was also an excellent engineer who provided all of our designs for the next two years. His first task was to redesign our transmitter, which was unreliable and difficult to assemble. He took what was already the most powerful transmitter in the industry and made it better. He turned the cadillac of the industry into a tank! In addition to more rugged components, heat sinks, and a huge transformer, he added state-of-the-art lightning protection. Until then, we had used a Fi-Shock fence-charger housing, but with the new design, we created a housing of our own which used superior wire connectors and had slots to allow heat out. We began shipping this unit in the fall of 1992. Our transmitter was clearly light years ahead of anything the competition had, including Invisible Fence.

MORE GREAT PEOPLE

As has always been the case, our success was due more than anything else to great people. Considering that we were a start-up operating out of a doublewide, we were fortunate to find others who could share in the vision.

The first time I met Walt Frankewich was in Fi-Shock's parking lot where he and Larry Manning were conducting an interview on the rear bumper of a car. We talked awhile about the opportunities and the vision we had for the future. Walt decided to join us and has been with us ever since, now the most senior member of our engineering department.

Phil Greene had a more proper interview. Larry Manning recruited him from Visicon too. Larry had already completed the preliminary interview but wanted me to visit with Phil. For better or worse, Phil recalls having the impression that we were a very casual company by our meeting. I was in shorts, had a tan, he says, and had my feet propped up. He concluded that this guy must never work! He took the job to oversee quality, and in spite of finding out that there was a little more work going on than met the eye, has been one of our most dedicated and hardworking associates ever since. He helped create our quality department, then later transferred to establish our call center, then even later went back to work within the quality department.

Yet another recruit from Visicon was Bill Groh. Bill was our first mechanical engineer. Since his start, he has had a hand in nearly every major product we have ever produced.

Renee Lane also started in 1992 along with Karrie Greene. Karrie started in our call center as one of our first consumer service representatives reporting to Phil (she later transferred to the sales department, married Phil, and he now reports to her). Renee worked for the cleaning company that serviced us, applied with Melanie, and became a key member of our accounting department and remained there until the year 2000.

Suzanne Sackleh joined us in 1992 and was our total art and graphics department for the next four years. She was talented and diligent but was also well-known for her own particular logic. For instance at the National Hardware Show in 1992, we all collected business cards and wrote comments on the back of them. Most comments usually read something like "100 stores, interested in Radio Fence, send quote, good prospect." As we were reviewing cards on the way back from the show one afternoon, we noticed one with the comment, "Nice Shoes." It was Suzanne's. Her logic was that if he had nice shoes, he was probably successful and thus worthy of serious follow-up. The following year when we introduced our bark collar, Suzanne buzzed me while working on the packaging inquiring whether we wanted to mention it could be used for cats similar to what we were then doing on the Radio Fence box. We decided not to do this. She was not only great fun but contributed greatly to the look and feel of Radio Fence.

Mary Lindsey, Robert Emory, and Mike Blalock also joined us that year. Mary has managed accounts receivable and watched our yearly revenues go from $4 million to $70 million. Robert started as an RMA clerk, then advanced to the position of repair technician and eventually moved into the engineering department, playing a key role in the development of new products.

The first two years were full of alternating, exciting wins and devastating catastrophes. We knew little and learned everything as we went. Yet we accomplished far more than any of us ever expected and built a vehicle to take us to even loftier heights. While we had many obstacles still to overcome, we could see over them and could begin to dream big.

Randy had survived the early years of his business, and I was very proud of him. Only 50% of new businesses survive their first five years. These are the tough times, and usually it means sacrificing everything to succeed. You can't count hours; you simply must give it your all. I understood the strain that put him under, but also a person who is truly an entrepreneur will, with all the hardships incurred, still make these the most enjoyable years of their lives. It's called "survivor bragging rights."

I believe this is a textbook for anyone desiring to try on his own in creating and building a business. The following is a story of what it takes to build a great company, its hardships, and rewards.

Have no illusions; being an entrepreneur is not for everyone.

A FATHER'S SON

CHAPTER 6

A YEAR OF CHANGE

COMPETITION, TECHNOLOGY, AND GROWTH

Bill Clinton was president and Al Gore was vice president. Inflation was 2.69%, and the Dow was at 365. The average interest rate was 6%. 76 people died in the Waco siege. The European Union set up a free-trade zone. Gas had surpassed the $1 mark at $1.16, and a theater ticket was $4.14.

The value of one dollar then is worth $1.69 in 2018.

The year 1993 was a watershed one for the company. We came under our most serious attacks from many new, low priced competitors; we "discovered" China and outsourcing; and we developed a new technology. How we would use it would fundamentally determine our future.

It was also the year that we changed our name from Radio Fence Corporation to Radio Systems Corporation. Until then we were a single-product company. However, by 1993 we had aspirations for developing a range of electronic training products from bark control collars to remote trainers. These weren't long-deliberated strategic categories but simply insightful reactions to customer demand. Our retailers wanted more products from us. They were either carrying or were familiar with these other electronic products and told us the kind of things we liked to hear such as "If you make them, we will buy them."

Our first new product was the BC100 Bark Control Collar developed by Joe Babb. It used a vibration-sensing device similar to that of DT Systems and Tri-tronics. Like theirs, it was fraught with bark detection discrimination issues. But it was less expensive and smaller than the competition and got us underway into a category that would soon generate our highest volume in units. While a new product was important, our year was defined more than anything else by new competition.

NEW COMPETITION TAKES AIM

In 1991 and the first half of 1992 while we had many challenges pioneering the DIY pet containment category, the one saving grace was that we had no competitors at retail. All that changed in the second half of 1992.

Just as we were beginning to get some of the early problems to a manageable level, a new threat appeared. In the late fall of 1992, a product called "Hidden Fence" entered the market. This brand was being sold by a fairly infamous but successful pioneer of imported ceiling fans. At that time we were selling our one and only model for $275. The "Hidden Fence" was being offered for around $120. They had great contacts with the home center industry and quickly lined up a great set of reps.

Based on our success, they won many retailers that we had been trying to sell but couldn't because of our high price. By the spring of 1993, they had landed many marquis accounts, including Builder's Square, Pergament, and Handy Andy. All have since been bought or liquidated, but in 1993 they represented 350, 50, and 120 stores, respectively, an enviable list of customers.

Retailers would listen to our story about quality and features. But, the competition was equally glib in assuring them that their product was just as good. And at $120 versus $275, the natural inclination of a buyer is to want to believe it's better to offer the lower price. Fortunately, our scaremongering presentation about how bad the competition was proved sufficient to keep the loyalty of our existing accounts. But we were losing the battle for the rest of the market.

A second company joined the fray, Waters Research, out of Elgin, Illinois around the first of 1993. Their product known as "No More Fence" was introduced at $110. Their owner had a slightly better product, and he and his representatives targeted the pet industry. Over the next two years, they picked up PETsMART, Sears, and PetStuff in Atlanta (later bought by PETsMART), just to name a few. All of these customers we battled mightily for, but lost out, again due to the price.

It got worse. In the spring of 1993, a product known as "K-9 Corral" entered the market. The company called International Development Corporation (IDC) was owned by a U.S. company, and the product was imported from China. They were offering a complete kit for $69, about $10 less than we had in materials and labor in our product.

We decided to do some research on IDC starting with a Dun and Bradstreet report. The company was a start-up, and there was no real information on them, so Dun and Bradstreet called them and asked questions for their file. To my chagrin, they told them it was Radio Systems requesting the report. For some reason, the company owner took this to imply that we might have interest in doing business with him and called and arranged an appointment.

I clearly remember the day we sat at a small table in my office, and he reviewed his product with me briefly. After a quick summary, he stated, "This is not rocket science; any idiot can design one of these." He offered to sell us a private label version for $50. I told him that I needed to have our engineer study it, and we would get back to him.

At the time our senior engineer was Joe Babb. I probably biased Joe unnecessarily by sharing with him the "any idiot" comment, and after a day of study, Joe came back and said, "Any idiot could have designed the K-9 Corral." And he was right. The receiver had a battery life of six to ten days and would false shock with the slightest sound. However, we were very concerned about their ability to sway buyers, get the product placed, and ruin the reputation of our fledgling and fragile market.

In spite of arguments about their poor quality, buyers wanted to believe that they would be OK with the cheapest priced product and greedily added the K-9 product. One of the largest customers they got was Target along with Payless-Cashways, Venture Stores, and Pamida.

As we grew, our vice president of sales proved less adept at selling to large retailers than he had been at setting up ASICs, although he was learning. I made all the key retailer calls and had the principal relationships with the reps. As our business grew from ASICs to more conventional channels of distribution, the plan was to get our head of sales more involved with them. Fortunately for Radio Systems, we hadn't made much progress in doing so.

In February of 1993, he was approached by Hidden Fence and offered twice his salary and 10% of their company to join them. They assumed that he had the relationships with the major retailers, which he didn't, and was responsible for our success at retail, which he wasn't. I tried to convince him that they were just using him and that his long-term prospects would be much greater at Radio Systems. I was unpersuasive, and he made the switch.

As you might imagine, having the company's VP-sales defect to the competitor at such a vulnerable time was potentially devastating. He was privy to all production, engineering, financial, and sales plans. All of us, and certainly I, felt betrayed. Not only was our company betrayed, but I felt our friendship was as well. Though I've read of many other companies where similar things have happened, it didn't make it any easier to take.

What did make it easier to take was winning. Our VP-sales defector and I had some major battles over key customers as a result, in particular, with Hechinger's. It's with some pride that I can say we won everyone, and within six months Hidden Fence let him go, and six months after that the company went out of business.

SELLING – WHY WE WERE BETTER

While the competition was fierce, we did win a lot of battles too. In 1993 we picked up some major new accounts. Lowe's added us that year on a ship-to-store basis. In the fall of 1993, we won the biggest retailer of all – Walmart.

Selling Walmart is an experience for most vendors, and we were no exception. By the time I called on them, I had been selling since I was 16, for about 18 years, so I had seen a few colorful characters and had some challenging selling experiences. But selling Walmart was then and still ranks as the most interesting, and in retrospect, the most fun.

My buyer was a seasoned veteran who has no equal. He is colorful, dynamic, and very dedicated. Though I had sent several letters and made several calls, I had never gotten a response from anyone at Walmart. Then out of the blue, I got a call from the buyer's assistant to set up an appointment. A store had called him and suggested he look into electronic containment systems. As with most buyers even at the largest chains, while they may not be responsive to vendors, they are very attentive to their store managers.

The meeting was in May of 1993, and the only product I had to offer was a $275 Radio Fence. The buyer listened to my presentation and bought into all the reasons why this category was not one where selling the cheapest product was wise. I argued about how the safety of the dog depended on the system, the terrible consequences of a poorly designed system that caused false shocks, and of the assurance that Underwriter's Laboratories would give his customers. Still he wasn't convinced it was a product for Walmart primarily due to the price. While demonstrating the features of the transmitter, he commented that he could buy televisions for less, and we had less parts, so we should be cheaper. I left him with his assurance that he would review the category in more depth in the fall and that he would consider us first and last when he did.

My next contact was in September of that year when he called to tell me he had looked at another brand, K-9 Corral, and was getting ready to put it in their stores but thought he'd give me one last chance! So much for having the inside track! Of course, I rushed down to see him the following week.

Since that first visit, we had introduced our first economy model, the RF1000, that we could sell for $125. It featured a new, smaller transmitter without all the features of our original transmitter but still sufficient for the average customer. With the new price, I had some reason for hope.

The competition had presented a $60 system and made compelling arguments, such as the fact that Target was carrying their product and Walmart would be embarrassed at retail if they couldn't sell a $99 unit. Of course, I drug out every scare-mongering tactic I could to try to persuade him that this category should be an exception to Walmart's normal practice of buying the lowest price.

At Walmart, there is a corridor off the lobby with about 30 or 40 very small meeting rooms. After about ten minutes and in the middle of my presentation, the buyer got up and with dramatic effect announced, "You've lost! You've lost it! I can't believe it. You've lost!" and walked out of the room. I sat there for a minute, stunned and dejected. Then awkwardly got up and looked down the corridor. There were no buyers, just dozens of other vendors having their surely more successful meetings in the other little rooms. After another minute to recover, I started to pick up my samples and put them back in my box. As I was doing this, the buyer came back into the room with vendor forms and sat back down at the table. "With these forms, you will be a vendor of Walmart. I don't care what you've heard about Walmart; we are a great partner and will work together on building this category. Now that doesn't mean that if this thing really takes off, I'm not going to come back to you and ask for another 25% discount. But we're loyal. Let's start with a 400-store test."

He passed some vendor forms over and reviewed them with me. Then he took my quote and marked through some of the prices, giving himself about a 10% to 15% discount. I told him there was no way we could do that and thought that was crystal clear. He handed me the product forms to fill out and let me know that he had a big store managers' meeting in a few weeks, and I needed to get him samples and a display, which I did.

After the meeting, I was at first disappointed. I had hoped to get the entire chain. However, it gradually sunk in that a 400-store test still represented more stores than any other retailer I had ever sold. For a young company just getting started, calling on and then selling Walmart was a very big event, and all of the people at Radio Fence were very excited when I returned with the news.

However, much to my surprise, the selling had just begun. To insure there was no mistake, I resent my quote to the buyer when I returned along with the completed item forms. About a month later, he was in Tulsa presenting our products to the store managers in a tradeshow, booth-type setting. His assistant called me at the office and said that she had faxed him the product forms and that the prices weren't what we had agreed to! He was too busy with the show to call during the day but wanted my home number, which I gave to her.

Having a Walmart buyer calling me at home was a pretty big honor, I thought. He called me at home about 10:00 p.m. and first told me that the stores loved the display and the products, so much so that he decided he wanted to roll it out to even more stores. But he said, "Randy, Randy, what are you trying to do to me! We agreed on a price and then you sent in the product forms with a much higher price. How can I trust you if you are going to do things like this to me? I must have the price we agreed on." I explained to him that we had not agreed on these lower prices and that I had sent a confirmation back to him over 30 days earlier. He replied, "I don't pay attention to things like that; I had an understanding with you. Are you going to say no to the business?" Knowing our costs and what I knew we had to have to make a profit, I made one of the most difficult decisions I had ever had to make. I told Walmart no. This was unacceptable said the buyer. "Randy, this can be very big for your business. You can't tell me no. I want you to think about this. I'm going to finish this show and then call you next week, and we'll talk about it then." I assured him I wouldn't change my mind, but I'd be glad to talk to him.

Needless to say, I was devastated. I called my father the next day, and he assured me that it was the right thing to do as did the rest of my management team. I didn't see any reason to delay my response, and the day after his call, I typed a letter telling him that we could only agree to the pricing I had offered before and that we were saying no to his proposal. I included copies of the original documents showing that we never agreed to any lower pricing. I had said no to Walmart, the largest retailer in the world. I knew that they could have possibly doubled our business, but more volume with too little margin would not have done us any good. Still, to have won the account and then to have to say no to it was difficult.

On Friday of the following week, the buyer called. He had just gotten back from the meetings and asked me for my decision. "Didn't you get my letter?" I said. "Yes, but I threw it away. You didn't really mean it. Randy, let's do some business. Honor our agreement, and let's get started." After another agonizing 30 minutes on the phone, we finished again with my saying no. Once was hard, the second time in writing was harder, and now a third time! Though I was now practiced at it, it was nonetheless depressing each time.

That night I had dinner at home, depressed and fatigued, I shared the story with my wife. She consoled me that the buyer was surely crazy and that I had done the right thing. We turned in early and around 9:30 I was with my son, Thomas, reading him a bedtime story, half asleep myself. The phone rang. My wife answers from our bed and says, "Randy, it's for you. I think it's that guy from Walmart." It was. This time he and I must have talked for an hour, me explaining why I couldn't give him the discounts and him explaining how he couldn't buy at our price. Finally I gave in. Partially. We agreed the kit price would remain the same, but I reduced the cost of the extra receiver from $30 to $25 (where it has stayed for all of our customers ever since).

And with that, we became a Walmart vendor. While it was a tortuous ordeal, I have great respect to this day for our buyer. He was dedicated and tenacious, working all hours of the day and night to put together the program he felt he needed. Less than a year later, he was promoted, and we have had a succession of other buyers, but I still believe he may have been the best I've ever dealt with anywhere. He definitely was the most colorful!

In 1992, Comtrad Industries out of Midlothian, Virginia contacted our VP of sales at a trade show. Our VP came back telling me how this company would advertise our product in an "infomercial and in print" for us if we would sell them product at our cost. It didn't sound like a very profitable proposition, and I said no. After he left us in early 1993, the prospect contacted me directly. They explained how they got remnant space from magazines and paid them with a percent of their sales, usually 33%. They argued that they could get circulation in the millions in major magazines. Their argument was persuasive, and we decided to give them a try though we did mark the product a slim 20%, not selling at cost.

Initially we had them promote our only Radio Fence product, the RF301, for $499. It failed miserably. However, by June of 1993, we had our new Standard Radio Fence, which we sold wholesale for $125 and sold to them for about $90. They advertised the product for $199, and demand exploded! They began selling 500 units a week by September and got us tremendous visibility. However, it was a double-edged sword. Buyers thought it was our company advertising. Many complained, and we had to explain that the advertiser was a separate company. But more importantly, we had literally tens of millions of ads throughout the country promoting our product and brand. They did more for our awareness over the next 12 months than anyone or anything before or since.

THE BEGINNING OF PETSAFE, LTD.

As a result of a Comtrad ad, an Englishman living in Beverly Hills got interested in the product and approached his close friend in the U.K., who was a managing director of Abercrombie and Kent, a travel agency. Together they decided to start up a business to promote our product concept in the U.K. They met with Invisible Fence, Innotek, and finally Radio Systems. They chose us because a) Invisible Fence couldn't make a decision, and b) they thought a lot of the professionalism of Larry Manning, our VP operations.

For us, they had money and were willing to dedicate resources in a market we had no hope of investing in ourselves for many years to come.

We signed an agreement in the fall of 1993 and began shipping to them the following year.

One of our U.K. customer's many talents was coming up with names. They decided to rename our product "Freedom Fence" because they thought Radio Fence was too technical and descriptive. One night over dinner, one of the partner's wife suggested the name "PetSafe" for the company name. Four years later, we would spend $30,000 and six months in market research to determine the best brand name for our product line and arrive at the same name that she did in five minutes!

DISCOVERING CHINA: OR RANDY AND HOWARD'S BIG ADVENTURE

I'm often asked how we got started with outsourcing in China. How does one find OEM manufacturers? How do you get started with them? Did we have someone that helped us make the introductions?

Fortunately, all the new Chinese-made knock-offs of our product were very poorly designed. Still we were amazed at how inexpensive they were. There was no way we could make product, even bad product, that cheaply. It was clear that there was something to manufacturing in China that we needed to explore. At the time Howard Fehl was our sole purchasing agent. He and I decided we needed to go to China and find out if there were any opportunities for us. We had always had our circuit boards contracted with outside suppliers and thought they would be the best parts to shop first.

Howard did all the groundwork. He found an organization called the Hong Kong Trade Development Council and let them know of our needs. They sent information on dozens of electronic OEMs, he made inquiries and set up appointments, and in January of 1993, Howard and I set off on a two-week exploratory trip.

In the first week, we met on average three factories a day, mostly in Hong Kong, but also made a couple of factory visits. During that week we met two companies, TOMCO and SUGA, both vendors of ours to this day. After the first week, we narrowed down our prospects to a list of about ten and the second week did factory visit after factory visit. As anyone who has done this knows, it was grueling. We'd meet for breakfast at 6:00 and review notes, then get picked up by the factory's salesman at 7:00 and head into China, a three-hour journey on average. Then we would tour a factory, have lunch, get passed to another salesman to take another factory tour, then trek back to Hong Kong in time for a late-night dinner with another potential factory. Afterwards we'd review the day's visits, handwrite faxes back to the office, and turn in around midnight. The next day we would do it all over again. While it wasn't nearly as glamorous as some think, we were thrilled. Yes, it was an exotic locale, and both Howard and I thrive on new, strange food. But the really exciting part was the pricing. On the Friday of the first week, Tomco gave us a quote of $9 for a receiver circuit board that we were buying for $26 in the U.S. Suga gave us a slightly higher price, but based on their superior capabilities, we decided on them for this product. Everything from batteries to wall adapters was quoted at savings from 40% to 70% less than we were used to paying. We spent quite a bit of time understanding how it was all possible from lower labor to lower overhead. Like most making their first visit, we were overwhelmed.

At the end of the second week on the Friday morning before we departed, a British gentleman came to visit us at our hotel. He represented Santai, a company that did everything from adaptors to plastics to PCBA assembly. We didn't have time to do a factory visit but planned a follow-up trip to do so. Santai eventually went out of business, but we followed the British gentleman to a new supplier, Whitways, a year later and have had a relationship with him and that company since.

After the first visit, we decided to give a contract to Suga on receiver circuit boards, Santai on adaptors, and also sourced a few other parts such as batteries. I made a second trip over on my own two months later and selected Santai for our transmitter circuit boards. Between Howard and I, we made seven trips in 1993 researching dozens of leads on OEMs, both in China and Taiwan. After more factory tours than we can recount, we had selected a core group of suppliers that we felt confident in, and gradually by the end of the summer, virtually all our circuit boards, batteries, adaptors, and probes were being sourced in Asia.

Since they have been such an integral part of our history, I should share a little about two of our most important partners, Suga and Whitways. We met Suga on the very first visit and left feeling they were the best match for us. At the time, they had revenues of around $10 million and had 400 employees to our $5 million and 150 employees. They had some major customers, such as Canon and Citizen, and had very modern facilities equal to or superior than any of our suppliers in the U.S. The workforce all seemed motivated and happy, even the line workers, something I seldom noticed in our U.S. suppliers' assembly areas.

The founder and CEO of the company, who owned 45% of Suga, was a Ph.D. and former university professor in electronics. He had spent considerable time in the U.S. and Japan, and he and I have had many interesting discussions regarding business management. He blends what he feels is the best of American, Japanese, and Chinese management theory at Suga. He is a very thoughtful, caring, and astute businessman.

Management owned another 6%, and a consortium of major electronics firms owned the balance. In short, Suga was a well-managed, modern company that had the quality we needed but wasn't so large that our business wasn't important to them. Partially as a result of our partnership but more as a result of their management, they have continued to grow, and as of this writing, their sales have grown to over $80 million, and they now have close to 2,000 employees. It has been a great partnership, both growing together over the last nine years.

We didn't meet Whitways until mid-1994. Our friend left Santai and searched for a similar, multi-faceted factory and found Whitways. Whitways and its owner are very traditional Chinese with everyone in the family working in the company. The Owner is also very opportunity-focused, investing anywhere that there is a need, rather than being strategically driven.

As a result, Whitways has been able to supply us with diverse and ever-growing capabilities, from injection molding to tooling to extruded aluminum to, of course, electronic assembly. In the Chinese style, Whitways re-invests everything into its business, making it stronger so that they can pass it on to their children. Thus, there is a very strong, natural tendency to operate for the long term, which is a trait that has made them a great partner.Further, I should note that in our early days, we owed our very existence to Whitways and their owners. As was often the case in those formative years, we were short on cash. Time and again, Whitways sympathized with my pleas and bet on us, supplying us with product even though we were very far behind and very much over any reasonable credit limit.

I remember one day vividly. I was returning home from the Consumer Electronics Show in Las Vegas in January of 1995. We were completely out of transmitter circuit boards,and couldn't ship to anyone. Without shipping we had no hope of getting additional cash. However, we owed Whitways a substantial amount, all past due, and had no cash to pay them. I called their financial manager from a pay phone at the Las Vegas airport and pleaded my case. While she is a very cautious, hard-nosed financial manager, she must have decided we were a good bet and let the shipment of transmitters go. If she hadn't, it is very likely we would be a much different company today.

I often hear people make derogatory comments about Chinese manufacturing. However, I could not disagree more strongly. Our quality improved dramatically, from 30% reject rates with our U.S. suppliers to less than 2% in the same year with our overseas suppliers. Their reliability was also far superior. I can't recall the number of times I was misled by some of our local OEMs regarding shipments. Once I visited one in Soddy-Daisy, Tennessee that had promised to ship 1,000 transmitter boards on a Tuesday. On Wednesday when we hadn't received them, I drove down to visit them unannounced and found that not only were they not shipping, they didn't even have the parts to start assembly!

While it is true that the pricing is a great attraction, the reliability, the quality, and true partnership our vendors in Asia have shown us would still make them our partners of choice. And it was due to the prices and service that they supplied in late 1993 that positioned Radio Systems for the explosion in growth that we experienced in 1994.

ASIC TECHNOLOGY REVOLUTIONIZES
OUR COMPANY

In late 1992, Bill Franklin introduced me to Dr. Ron Nutt of CTI. Bill told me that Ron had put together a very talented team of engineers that made VLSI chips (Very Large Scale Integrated), also known by another acronym, ASICs, for Application Specific Integrated Circuits. Ron's company made positive emulsion topography machines, a more dynamic version of a CAT scan, for the medical industry. Unfortunately the team Ron had put together was reaching the end of the project. He wanted to keep the team together, and when Bill heard this, he thought of us.

I met Ron one afternoon at his very spartan, practical offices. I explained the challenges of our Radio Fence receiver, those being noise rejection, battery consumption, and size. He confidently predicted that he could solve them all with an ASIC. Within a few weeks, we had worked out an arrangement.

Ron asked a reasonable price for the project, $300,000 ($537,000/2018) plus the set-up costs at the foundry, which was about another $75,000 ($134,000/2018). In addition, we paid a $3.50 ($6.27/2018) royalty on the first 100,000 chips that we bought. Ron set up a separate company, RKN, Inc., later changed to Concorde Microsystems, to do the development.

Ron liked our company but said he wouldn't be interested if he didn't have an equity stake in the company. At the time, I owned 100% of Radio Systems (and 100% of Saco) and wasn't particularly interested in parting with stock and hadn't even contemplated the eventuality, but we needed the technology, most critically the noise rejection that could eliminate false shocks, and the idea of cash for equity sounded good.

We were approaching $5 million ($8.9 million/2018) in sales for the year but just barely breaking even. Somehow, and frankly I forget how, we agreed on a valuation of $3 million ($5.37 million/2018) for the company. With that valuation, we agreed to take $75,000 ($134,250/2018) for 2.5% of the company and gave Ron an option to buy another 7.5% for $225,000

($402,750/2018) later if he chose. Thus Ron became our first shareholder other than me. Ron also joined the board of directors becoming its fourth member (my Dad volunteered to be corporate secretary and Todd Birdwell, my former banker, to be treasurer. We never met before Ron joined, but it was a state requirement to have some names on the corporate registration).

For the next year and a half, Joe Babb, our sole engineer, and the Concorde team, consisting of Jim Rochelle, Dave Bentley, Robert Nutt, Ron Nutt, and Brian Swann, toiled away. Since all had daytime jobs, meetings started after normal work hours and sometimes lasted until midnight. I sat in meetings to give some marketing direction but generally just listened. However, the promise of the technology was extremely exciting. By the fall of 1993, we were in position to start ordering production quantities of the ASICs.

The good news was that the ASIC delivered on every promise and more. A $26 circuit board with 55 analog components and a microprocessor could be replaced with a single 2.2 by 2.2-millimeter chip that cost $1.27 ($2.20/2018). The receivers could drop in size by half. Battery consumption, which was a sad industry standard of one $15 ($26.1/2018) custom battery every 30 to 60 days or over $100 ($174/2018) per year for the consumer, dropped to one six-volt alkaline battery at $2 ($3.48/2018) every 3 to 4 months. Reliability was increased too with one component replacing over 50. Most importantly, the principal problem that drove returns over 35% in 1993, false shocks due to our inability to screen out noise interference, was solved. Nothing would falsely set off this new ASIC! This one feature would be the most significant reason for our success in the coming years and one of the main reasons for so many other companies' failures.

The bad news was that I had no money to pay Concorde when the time came to do so. Ron was probably aware of our continuing cash flow problems, being on the board as he was. However, without Ron's help, we would not be able to pay for the technology. We agreed to sell Ron the other 7.5% of the stock for $225,000 ($391,500/2018), some of which went to pay for the set-up costs to the foundry, a company called Orbit in Sunnyvale. We also negotiated to trade Concorde, now owned by the engineers and Ron's son, Robert, for the balance of what we owed them in stock.

At the time, they had put a lot of time and effort into a project along with some cash to subcontractors and got in return some equity in a two and half year-old company with incredibly high returns, one product, no financing, and one that had never turned a material profit. I would like to think that it's turned out to be a good bet for them with a return of around 20 times their investment, one that would be worth over $8 million ($13.9 million/2018) today – not too bad for part-time work for a year.

This same investment in 2017 was worth over 200 times the original. Quite a return.

But they deserved it. They took a big risk on a small start-up and provided a technology that few in the world could have.

MANY NEW KEY ASSOCIATES JOIN THE TEAM

In 1993, we began working with Petco, a future perennial top-five customer. While at their trade show in August, I called in to find that my entire engineering team had just quit! Of course, there was only one electrical engineer at the time, Joe Babb. It was a very devastating loss.

Joe was kind enough to recommend an RF engineer named Alan Boardman who was quickly hired but could only work part-time, three days per week. I'll share more about Alan later. However, we had many ideas for new products and really needed to continue to improve our core Radio Fence product, so we launched an extensive search for another electronic engineer. Tum Sangsingkeow came recommended by Jim Rochelle. We made him an offer, and he accepted and has since become one of our most successful engineers, currently our senior engineer, with many of our key products to his credit.

Also in 1993, Steve Baker, Kevin Ogle, and Mike Blalock joined Radio Systems. Steve came to us by way of Larry Manning, having worked with Steve at their former company, Visicon. Steve was hired in to manage materials processing and was quickly recognized as one of the company's future stars. Kevin Ogle and Mike Blalock joined us that year as technicians and have continued to be great contributors to the company, from their roles then as technicians to leading our quality and returns areas.

NEW MONEY AND NEW FRIENDS

As a member of our board, Ron recognized that we needed additional equity to manage our growth. With his assistance, we managed to secure our first, real bank relationship through Third National Bank. Sure, I had to pledge my home and everything else they could think of, but they did advance us a $400,000 ($696,000/2018) line of credit based on the level of our receivables and inventory.

Ron also introduced us to Otto Wheeley that fall. Otto was a former University of Tennessee graduate who went on to great success at Koppers in Pittsburgh, retiring as the vice deputy chairman. He was unarguably the most active venture capitalist in East Tennessee.

Otto has been a key to our success ever since. For those that don't know him (and I think that would be few, as it seems he knows everyone), Otto is the most tireless, energetic, and enthusiastic person one could ever hope to meet. He is one of the few people that accuse me of being too conservative and unambitious. As of this writing Otto is 82, and occasionally I'll have people say that they hope to have his energy when they are his age. My sincere response is "I wish I had his energy at any age."

Otto introduced us to Tennessee Innovation Center, an investment fund of Lockheed Martin, one they were required to set up to fund Tennessee start-ups as a requisite for them getting the contract to manage Oak Ridge National Laboratories. The fund was being managed by Mel Koons, who later became our corporate secretary. Mel liked the company and agreed to invest $400,000 ($696,000/2018) into RSC, buying shares at $3 ($5.22/2018) per share.

Mel served us well as corporate secretary guiding us through the necessary legal formalities of running a growing company. He also acted as our counsel in the purchase of Austin Innovations assets in 1996 and the marketing agreement with Multivet Ltd. in 1997, in both cases saving us lots of money. It was a very sad day in 2001 when Mel passed away. We should not forget his contributions and support.

Otto also introduced us to the Tennessee Center for Research and Development, had a fund with money from the state of Tennessee and TVA, the fund being called "Beta Development." Mike Howard, who became a longtime supporter and friend of Radio Systems, managed the fund. Beta also invested $200,000 ($348,000/2018). Otto put together a fund of his own, NSBW, the initials of his children, and invested $100,000 ($174,000/2018). All told, 17.5% of the company had been sold.

This infusion of cash was desperately needed and enabled us to survive and grow for the next year. While we may have managed without it, we would be a far smaller and very different company than we are today. Besides cash, these investors also brought tremendous expertise, and their guidance proved invaluable over the years.

Update 2018 – Otto died in 2012 at the age of 90. I will always remember his advice about having a great team. He would advise in parables. My favorite one – "If you see a turtle on top of a fence post, he didn't get there by himself."

WATERSHED MEETING – A BOUTIQUE OR MASS BRAND?

With the ASIC, we were presented with one of the most important decisions that we had yet to make and arguably the most important in our history. The ASIC, combined with the China sourcing, had dropped our overall costs by over 50%. We were selling the Deluxe for $275 ($478/2018) and the Standard for $125 ($217/2018). With the new costs, we could hold pricing, make a substantial margin, and support it with our clearly superior technology.

However, we were losing market share and fast. Hidden Fence was selling a complete system for around $80 ($139/2018), No More Fence for around $70 ($122/2018), and K-9 Corral for around $55 ($96/2018). Retailers were convinced that the magic retail price point was $99 ($172/2018). We were maintaining the loyalty of our existing customers but not winning many new ones.

Besides losing market share, we were very concerned about the future of our industry. The other products simply did not work, having all of the problems we did early on but without the margin or infrastructure to make up for it. And they were selling them at much higher volumes than we had in our early days. Yet consumers considered the products generic, and we worried that for every bad experience, there would be ten or maybe even a 100 potential customers who would be turned off from any brand, retailers would drop the product, and the category would be killed at retail. Our competitors were all importers with skeleton staffs and looking for a fast buck; we were building our future on the electronic containment category.

Larry Manning, Melanie Thomas, Howard Fehl, and I had a fateful meeting at a local grill for lunch late fall of 1993 where we debated the issue. We had the ability to fight the competition by coming close to their price and with the superior technology, take back our market share and potentially eliminate them as competitors, thus protecting our industry. To hit a retail of $99 ($172/2018), we would have to take the wire and flags out of the kits, but that would allow us to sell them for $60 ($104/2018) and $120 ($208/2018), respectively. Besides, when we got product returns, the wire was never returned with the kit. Thus, this would also reduce the cost of returns. We did offer a version with wire for $20 ($35/2018) more, but most of the sales were for kits packaged without wire.

Today this might sound like an easier choice than it appears. We were still in a continual state of back order, and our biggest issue was trying to fill orders. My principal occupation was trying to appease upset customers (and sell vendors on extending more credit to us). To make the same gross margin and revenues in 1994 at these new prices, we would have to sell twice as many units.

We took the aggressive position, changed our pricing, and prepared for the challenges ahead. Nothing great ever came from being timid; taking the bold course of action has and will continue to define our company.

Note from Tom Boyd: Randy had surpassed the big hurdles of business and was ready to explode on a bigger screen. Meanwhile Fi-Shock had a product that did the same thing but required an above-ground wire. Randy had seen the future, and we had not. He knew there was a market for pet containment. So did I, but what our company had overlooked was that very few wanted an unseemly, wire fence running around their yard. His product eliminated that, and they went on to capture the market, and we lingered on that product at around $1 million in sales. The following pictures capture the transition. I always hated to lose, but in this instance, I was overjoyed with my competitor's success.

Tom Boyd, president of Fi-Shock, holds a control box his company makes to deter pets, keeping them in or out of a specific area by giving an electrical shock when attached wires are touched.

This was a featured story in the *Knoxville News Sentinel* in 1993, a year before the next story on Randy in 1994. As easily seen, he exceeded what we were doing with our product.

Amy Geisel, business writer wrote – Fi-Shock, Inc. sells its products in South Africa to keep crocodiles from killing goats, in southern Georgia to keep chickens from defecating in their feed. Boyd said their sales were $10 million.

Randy Boyd, president of Radio Systems Corp., holds a card showing the size of the company's old transmitter on the left and the new, much smaller transmitter on the right. Boyd says RadioSystems makes the smallest radio dog collar in the business.

This story was in the *Knoxville News Sentinel* in 1994 written by Amy Geisel, the same writer that wrote the story on me the year before. Her quote from the article is below.

"Randy Boyd, the company's founder and president, expects sales in 1994 to top $23 million, more than double 1993 sales of $9 million. In 1995, Boyd unflinchingly says, the company will post sales of $50 million plus."

— Amy Geisel

"Randy always dreamed big, and in fact, beat this projection." — Tom Boyd

CHAPTER 7

A YEAR OF GROWTH, EXPANSION, AND DIVERSIFICATION

With our new pricing, new products, and new packaging, we went to market in 1994 needing to double our unit sales to just maintain our revenue dollars. Of course, we wanted to do more than just stay even. And we did. In fact, we managed to quadruple unit sales and double dollar sales in 1994, a 100% increase. Production ran 24-hours a day, and we expanded to over 150 associates, most of them in assembly. And while producing enough product to meet demand was still a challenge, some of our other problems were minimized, in particular our quality. With the advent of the ASIC, most of our quality problems with our receiver were eliminated. It was also a great year in many ways, with tremendous gains in market share, exceptional new associates, and new, value-added investors.

MANY NEW FACES

Radio Systems has been a success due to its many dedicated, intelligent, and hardworking associates. We hear of college football teams talking about their recruiting class, and in 1994
we had a great one, a full parade of All-Americans.

Jim Hudson joined the team. In the first three years in business, one of my most important jobs was deciding who was to get paid. This is a very difficult chore when you only have enough money to pay about half of what you need to do. On average, I would spend as much time in a week selling vendors on continuing to ship to us as I did on selling new customers.

Another major vocation was prospecting banks and investors and then keeping them happy. Not having the confidence and the casual atmosphere we enjoy today, many of us were in suits and ties most days as we tried to impress some financial visitor.

Our biggest frustration was that our accounting capabilities were such that we never knew whether we were making money or not. We would show a huge profit one month and then a huge loss the next on roughly the same sales. We had adopted MAS90 software the previous year on Larry Manning's suggestion, but we didn't have the proper accounting personnel to create reliable financial statements. Of course, such erratic reporting exacerbated our money raising attempts and didn't provide much confidence for our board.

By late 1993, the board insisted that I find a "chief financial officer," and they all began helping me search. There were many interviews, but it was difficult to find the high caliber person we needed, who was entrepreneurial enough to join what was still virtually a start-up. The candidate would need to have top management skills to take us where we needed to go but must be willing to roll up their sleeves and do some basic accounting, work that they would have probably advanced beyond years earlier in their career.

In the spring of 1994, my board friend, Todd Birdwell, had an acquaintance who knew a man named Jim Hudson and recommended we meet with him. Jim came in one morning and interviewed with me for about two hours. He didn't seem in a hurry to leave, so he was invited to a company luncheon we were having to celebrate something, I forget what. He and the rest of the team interacted well, and I'd like to think Jim liked the atmosphere and energy of our little company.

Why Jim over any of the other candidates? In the interview, he told me how vendors need to buy into the dream and how they should invest in us. He'd obviously been down this road before. There were plenty of candidates who could have straightened out the accounting department but very few that could adopt and then sell our vision. Jim could. To make a long story short, after another month of conversations and follow-up, Jim came to work with us in April of that year. I'm overjoyed to say that I haven't had to make any accounts payable decisions or take a delinquent account call since. While I didn't always like our financial results, they were accurate and understandable.

A vice president of quality – Lin Tisdale. With our many quality troubles, it became critical that we place special emphasis on this key part of our business. As part of this effort, we all took a total quality management class and were very impressed with the instructor, Dr. Lin Tisdale. We were so impressed that we hired him as our vice president of quality. Lin was only with us for a year. He proved to be a great instructor but not a hands-on implementer of procedures. Still, we learned a lot from him.

Lin had many analogies, and my favorite is one I've repeated many times. Lin described these campers on the side of a river just above a waterfall. They noticed someone floating down the stream heading for the precipice. They quickly devised a way to rescue the person. Shortly thereafter, another person came floating down the river, and they saved him too. Soon more and more people were floating downstream, and the campers developed a very elaborate and efficient way of pulling them out of the stream. Lin would share this story and then point out, "What they should be doing is finding out why so many people were falling into the stream in the first place!" I share this story because it is so important, and while this analogy seems funny and obvious, similar scenarios play out in business every day. Too often we are consumed with developing means to solve the symptoms when we should be focusing our efforts on the causes.

Barbara Thompson – VP– children's products division. We realized early on that our products could be leveraged for other uses beyond just managing pets. One application was to use the fence product to notify a caregiver, either a parent or someone monitoring an Alzheimer's patient, if they left the yard. Barbara Thompson was recruited to lead this division.

Barbara had a very successful career by founding start-ups in educational children's toys. She brought many ideas to us about how to write product specifications, conduct focus groups, and the value of packaging to attract the consumer. Unfortunately, we did not have the engineering resources to dedicate to both the children's products and the pet products, and Barbara became very frustrated with having to always wait behind a pet project. She left us two years later in January of 1996, and with her left any attempts to address the children's products' market. While the potential is still there, the concern then, as now, is that it is difficult to go in two separate directions simultaneously and effectively, and we concluded that we would be best served doing one thing well, and that one thing for Radio Systems is pet products.

MARKETING SUCCESSES AND FAILURES

In 1994, I was the entire sales team. Every week was another three or five-day trip introducing our new products. However, it was a role that I would not have wanted to share with anyone. These presentations were every salesman's dream! It went something like this. I had a new receiver that was half the size of the former unit, drained one fourth the power, and now used commonly accessible batteries. They also no longer were set off by false signals. The packaging was vastly improved with great graphics, the customer hotline number on the front, and nicely shrink-wrapped.

After awing the customers with the improvements, I then announced the price of the deluxe kit would drop from $275 ($464/2018) to $125 ($211/2018), and the standard kit would drop from $125 ($211/2018) to $60 ($101/2018)! Watching the customers' expressions was always a lot of fun. We were heroes, and the customer got very excited about all the promotional opportunities the new pricing created. We were already a major hit anyway, and with these product and pricing windfall improvements, they all saw the tremendous, new potential.

One change that had to be explained was the new concept of having the wire and flags packaged separately. Our logic was as follows. First, the average customer used 1,100' of wire, so including a 500-foot roll didn't meet the customers' needs anyway. Second, comparing the category to electric fencing, it was pointed out that people normally didn't expect to buy all the system components in one package. Lastly and importantly, by taking out the wire and flags, it allowed the retailers to promote a $99 ($169/2018) retail with a 40% margin.

Not all retailers went along. Kmart, who we had been wooing for several years, suddenly became interested with the new pricing. They had seen our product in 1992 but refused to pay $275 ($492/2018). I remember very clearly our former buyer showing up at our booth at the American Pet Products Manufacturers Association show in Orlando in 1992, drunk and yelling at me that if I didn't lower my price, he would develop knockoff products himself. And he did. In 1993, he sponsored a good friend into the business.

He had his friend's company, American Pet Products (that imported everything from China), a supplier of car mats and pet beds almost exclusively for Kmart, make a fence kit for him for around $60 ($104/2018). He introduced this product in Kmart in 1993.

With our new features and pricing, the Kmart buyer began to see the merit in a U.S.-made product with superior features. He was also experiencing high returns with the American Pet Products fence, but I didn't know that at the time. However, he insisted wire and flags be included (as had Walmart and Ames). The price with wire and flags increased to $80 ($139/2018). Ames still ran ads that spring at $89 ($155/2018) with wire and flags. However, Kmart said they wanted to be at $99 ($138/2018) and had to have a 30% margin. The buyer guaranteed me a 10,000-unit order if I would give him a $70 ($122/2018) price. Contrary to my agonizing debate with Walmart the year before, I gave in on the spot.

This was around January of 1994. Kmart took product in March and had their first big ad planned for the last of April. Two weeks prior to it, I found out that they were going to run the ad at $79.99 ($135/2018), less than I was selling product for others. I panicked and begged them to raise the price. Of course, they wouldn't listen. As a result and to pre-empt the backlash from other mass merchants like Ames and Walmart, we offered a promotional price to them of $70 ($118), a price that has remained to this day.

Needless to say, when the $79 ($133/2018) price hit the streets, all hell broke loose. Customers called from everywhere to scream at us. I hope we learned a couple of lessons from the experience, the first of which was to treat all customers fairly. The market place is too transparent, and if one customer gets a better deal than another, all will know about it. This pricing strategy has served us well with the exception of the two-step distributors, who traditionally insisted on better pricing in spite of lower volumes. Second, we learned to set a price and stick with it. This was a maxim we knew, broke, and had to relearn. Negotiating major price reductions with a single customer can cost much more than it can make.

We also experienced a problem that we wouldn't rectify for another two years. Having only one brand is very costly. Our flag ship premium brand was also our low cost, mass merchant "fighting" brand. It is impossible for one brand to serve both purposes.

This was also a big year for expansion into new accounts. Many retailers that weren't in the category before, added it, and we won many of the battles. We picked up Rickel's, half of Builder's Square, Fred Meyer in the Northwest, and many others. I was particularly proud of Rickel's, a 30-store home center chain in New Jersey, because the buyer's husband was the rep for a competitor, but she chose our product over his brand!

In spite of our sales success, we were still very focused on the competition, recognizing the fact that while our improvements were significant in the category, we still had seven other major competitors fighting for each account, all but one of which was less expensive than Radio Systems.

Can you say "Markdown money?" Not everything was perfect in those new pricing presentations, however. The Home Quarters buyer's enthusiasm lasted for about two seconds until he realized he had 4,000 kits in stock at the old price. What was he going to do with that now obsolete and overpriced inventory? In my inexperience, I assumed they would happily sell through it, and then put in the new product. That's not how they saw it. Instead I was offered two choices – buy all the existing inventory back or offer markdown money. This was an unexpected turn of events. And it was one that played out the same across the country. By the time the dust settled, we had had to offer over $500,000 in markdown money that spring. We learned that cost decreases to customers are not necessarily good things and have since opted for new product offerings rather than replacements at lower costs.

There were a few failures too. While we chalked up a lot of successes in 1994, we also lost a couple of key battles including PetSmart and Sears.

The Sears buyer had a close relationship with one of the competitors, Waters Research, based in Elgin, Illinois. Their product was the best of the low-cost imports though it still had significant problems such as high battery drain and false shocking. Partially due to the relationship, partly due to a very inept sales representative I had at the time (he wrote the chairman of Sears complaining that the buyer wasn't paying attention to pet products, a letter which filtered back to the buyer and didn't earn our representative any points), and due to the lower Waters' price, we lost the account.

At PetSmart, our buyer had not been in the category before, thinking the product was too DIY-oriented and too expensive. Now with all the lower pricing, they decided to get into the category. He was very concerned about the fact that the Radio Systems brand was sold in so many places, especially Kmart and Walmart. Nonetheless, we were in the running until the Kmart ad broke at $79. Shortly afterwards, they selected Waters Research too and their brand "No More Fence."

Waters became our most difficult competitor that year, landing not only Sears and PetSmart but also a part of the Builder's Square business, Pergament, and Handy Andy, all marquis home center chains at the time.

Pergament, Handy Andy, and Builder's Square are now all out of business.

PETSAFE, LTD TAKES OFF

Meanwhile across the Atlantic, PetSafe, Ltd., our new partners for marketing in Europe, began importing in February. With a focus on installing dealers, they had built slowly but solidly. One of the highlights of my early years was visiting them in November of 1994 to meet their network of "regional representatives" or RRs during their first annual sales conference.

These were individuals they had recruited across the United Kingdom to sell and install "freedom fences," their name for a Radio Fence. By a fluke in the way they networked, nearly all of their RRs were retired generals and executives from large corporations doing this for a little pocket money on the side. It made for a very distinguished group.

By the time of this first annual conference, they had over 30 RRs, and most had been selling the product for several months. Here we were, a company just a little over three years old, and I was thousands of miles away addressing a large group of very professional people all dedicated and enthusiastic about our products. It was all very exciting.

David Rogers, the managing director, also let me know about a very pesky individual in Belgium. It seemed this guy was determined to buy from PetSafe, though David being somewhat conservative, wasn't prepared to launch into Europe. PetSafe, Ltd. finally relented; the gentleman from Belgium drove to England, paid cash for some product, loaded the product in his trunk, and began marketing in Belgium. We had our first continental customer.

He named his new company New Best, which was a side business for him. His primary business was wholesaling precious gems. He would do demonstrations at his house on Saturdays, take orders, and have his sons go out and install them during the week. From this humble beginning, New Best is now one of our largest distributors anywhere in the world, servicing the Benelux and Germany. And I'm proud to say, this "gem" allowed him to discontinue the other business.

MEETING DEMAND

Of the challenges in 1994, once again just meeting demand was the most critical one. By this time, we had some of the nation's largest retailers buying from us, customers I was in awe of and proud to have acquired, such as Home Depot and Walmart. Comtrad, the direct response customer, was the first to offer the Radio Fence at $199, and they were selling over 1,000 pet containment systems a week by themselves.

As in 1992, demand greatly exceeded supply. Mondays would start with a succession of calls. "Hello, this is Walmart. I don't care what you do with any of your other customers, but no one back orders Walmart." "Hello, this is Home Depot. I don't care what you do with other customers, but no one backorders Home Depot. "Hello, this is Lowe's." "Hello, this is Kmart." And so on. We were only able to ship on average half of what was required, and in spite of the exhortations from these highly-valued customers, we did backorder them.

Many mail order customers, such as Foster and Smith, New England Serum, and R.C. Steele took over five years to forgive us. When they saw product on a retailer's shelves or saw a retailer's ad, they assumed we must be shipping those accounts at their expense. By the end of the year, we had lost all the major pet catalogs, opening the door to our rivals. To this day, we still have a very small share of the catalog market as a result.

The "war room." Every morning Howard Fehl, Larry Manning, Steve Baker, and a few others as needed would spend an hour or more planning the days' production strategy. Every angle was explored to expedite shipments. Often at great expense, we airfreighted nearly every component. These meetings went on for well over a year, and I will always remember the creative, imaginative, no excuses attitude of the group, constantly finding ways to squeeze out some small miracle each day.

At this time, we were also still doing final assembly, and we ran three shifts 24-hours a day. It was hard to sleep in those days worrying about the coveted customers I would be disappointing the next day. Often I would wake up in the middle of the night, give up on sleep, and drive to the factory. It was exhilarating to see 20 or 30 people on an assembly line at 3:00 a.m. working furiously to crank out your product. Unfortunately, the exhilaration usually wore off by the time the phones started ringing a few hours later.

PRODUCT DEVELOPMENT

In 1994, we launched many new projects. Although the products weren't introduced until 1995, most of the development work began in this year. Our efforts are best justified by one of our company values, "Try a lot of stuff and keep what works. Mistakes are recognized as a part of the learning and growing process." We tried a lot of stuff, most didn't work, but we grew as a company from the knowledge and experience of our mistakes.

A "wireless fence." "One of the most revolutionary and successful ideas we have had was one for a wireless pet containment system. However, it wasn't technically our idea. One day on a drive to a sales call with one of the salesman who worked for Bob Olson, our representative in Chicago, the salesman asked if one of our new products, Radio Repel, could be operated in reverse. While the dog was picking up the signal, he didn't get the correction. When he lost the signal, he would get the correction.

I thought about it for a moment and then, politely, explained why it was a stupid idea. First, the receiver would be receiving the signal all the time. We had been struggling for years to get battery life up. With the new ASIC, we were at three months. However, that assumed the dog would pick up the signal occasionally. For it to pick up the signal all the time would drain the battery in days, maybe hours, I stated. Further, the Radio Repel's maximum signal range was about 12', and I was told it would be very expensive to get any incremental distance. Thus, while I thanked him for the idea, I assured him it wouldn't work.

However, I kept thinking about the concept, and when I returned, I discussed it with Allan Boardman, the designer. Allan thought that he could manage the battery consumption issue by duty-cycling the receiver (having it come on and off periodically) and that he could get the range using a higher frequency radio signal. We decided to let him proceed.

He expected to have the product done by August and did have working prototypes by then. Alan was getting up to a 300' range which was great. Unfortunately, there was just one nagging problem that needed to be tweaked – the signal range was very volatile. If the weather changed or any object, for example the pet owner, got between the transmitter and the dog wearing the receiver, the range could be changed dramatically. Thus, one could set the range at 250', but in an instant it could drop to 50', then back again. Alan assured me that this was an easy fix, and he would have it solved in two weeks.

We decided to have the product photographed and put into the upcoming 1995 catalog. Parts were ordered for things that weren't expected to change like frequency crystals, plastic housings, etc. We were prepared to revolutionize the industry! In the fall, we began presenting them to our customers at $150 each. Everyone loved it. Ames agreed to buy 4,000 units on the opening order. Quality Stores was going to add eight per store. Comtrad, wanting to get a head start on the market, designed an ad to run in all the major magazines the first of January in 1995. As we will discuss later, investors poured money into the company because of this one product.

But in two weeks, Alan said it was going to be another two weeks. "Two weeks" became a rather humorless joke around the company as every time I asked for a status report, the answer was that it would be solved in two weeks.

By December we began to fear that this "minor problem" was not going to be solved. By January we were desperate. Comtrad could not pull back their ads, and many ran. The good news was that the "Wireless Radio Fence" was the most successful item Comtrad had ever run, outselling the previous best seller three to one. The bad news was we couldn't produce it.

Finally, Alan came to me and said that he couldn't solve this one "tweak," but otherwise the product worked perfectly and just as we had asked. I tried to explain that the dog getting random shocks every few minutes as the boundaries oscillated in and out was not acceptable. He left still thinking the product was a good design.

The lesson here is an obvious one – Every part of the product specification has to be met. We hit the cost targets and the range, but missed the ability to hold a tolerance. We miss one, and we don't have a product. We also didn't have a process or large enough team in place to have others critique a design.

In the end, with extreme embarrassment and cost, we had to discontinue the project, cancel customer orders, inform new investors, and eat the cost of all the materials we had ordered. But we didn't give up on the idea and began looking for alternative ways to produce it.

RADIO REPEL

The product development actually began in late 1993 and finished in early 1994. The "Radio Repel" was our first major new product. According to our consumer surveys, 47% of all dogs using a Radio Fence were primarily indoor dogs. This new product could keep the dog out of selected rooms or off furniture with the dog wearing the same outdoor Radio Fence collar. We were on pace to sell over 100,000 Radio Fence systems in 1994; thus, with an expected rate of one indoor system to every two outdoor systems, we ordered 5,000 per month for the next six months or 30,000 units. The good news is that the Radio Repel, now known as the Indoor Radio Fence, is one of the best functioning products we've ever made, and everyone that buys one loves it. The bad news is that customer demand, in spite of frequent name and packaging changes, has never met our expectations.

REMOTE TRAINING

The following year, 1995, was to be the year we launched into the remote training business. Only a percentage of dog owners needed a fence, but everyone had a training or obedience issue that could be solved with a trainer. We believed, and still do, that we could do for the remote training industry what we did for the pet containment industry. When we entered pet containment, there was only Invisible Fence selling through a limited distribution network of franchise installers and selling units at over $1,200 ($1,980/2018) installed. A company based in Tucson, Arizona, Tritronics, owned the remote trainer market. Their distribution was through a network of dealers and a few specialty mail order catalogs; they sold products for over $400 ($660/2018) and targeted primarily hunters. We believed we could take the product to the average pet owner, sell it for under $100 ($165/2018), and get mass distribution.

We developed two products. The first was an infrared remote trainer we called the "Good Dog Trainer." Ron Nutt introduced us to a contract engineer, Steve Zimmerman, who we hired to work on the project. Steve convinced us that infrared was a cheap and effective technology and that we could get a range of 100'. Unfortunately, the range was less than 30' in the best conditions, didn't work outside at all, and was very directional. If the dog wasn't facing you so that there was line of sight to the collar, it didn't work either. Unfortunately, we didn't discover these problems until we had launched the product the following year.

Meanwhile, Whitways was asked to develop a "Sport Dog" remote trainer. The spec was a) to transmit up to a half mile, b) train up to five dogs with five separate frequencies simultaneously, c) have eight levels of correction, and d) offer a positive tone, a negative tone, and shock. Whitways said they could deliver the product in four months and at a turn-key cost of $30 ($49/2018). We were going to offer it for $60 so that it could retail for $99 ($163/2018). We would again revolutionize an industry!

Unfortunately, Whitways never delivered. Month after month passed with due dates being missed for prototypes. By early 1995, they finally sent notice that the contractor they were using to develop the project had gone out of business. Again we promoted the product to the market and had a lot of egg on our face for not being able to deliver.

BARK CONTROL

Our first bark control collar was introduced in 1993, the BC100. It was huge and very sensitive. It shocked with virtually every movement of the dog. We sent relatively few out and got all of them back. We recognized that the most difficult spec for a bark collar was the accurate detection of the bark.

Steve Zimmerman had the idea of using voice recognition technology to record the exact bark pattern of the dog. Using a voice recognition chip and a microprocessor, this design could emit up to ten selectable levels of shock. The same button could be depressed and held to memorize the dog's bark. It was very complicated, and we had the highest non-defective return rates of any product we had developed. The product struggled on for another three years but was finally discontinued in 1997.

PRIVATE BROADCASTING SYSTEMS OR PBS

While we pursued new products, we had not learned the value of focus and pursued many product ideas in spite of our ability to market them. In our defense, we did not see ourselves solely as a pet company. In fact, the pet channel was a very small part of our business. And we really only had one successful product, a Radio Fence. We thus saw ourselves as a technology-based manufacturer of consumer electronics. It would be two years before we settled on the pet focus.

One of the more interesting tangents was PBS, the Private Broadcasting System. This device broadcast a message on an AM radio channel at very short range up to about 300' away. The market use was for retailers and real estate agents to post a sign telling the passerby to tune to a particular channel and then broadcast a prerecorded message on a digital voice chip. Walt Frankewich led this design and created a functional product. Unfortunately, we had limited success marketing the concept and decided, in the cut backs that would follow in the next few years, to jettison this product.

TRY A LOT OF STUFF AND KEEP WHAT WORKS

When we post this as a corporate value, it is not to be interpreted to mean "try a lot of products and keep what works." However, we did do a lot of that in the first few years. What it does mean is to learn from our mistakes and improve our processes. In 1994, we learned the value of field testing products thoroughly before launch. We learned the importance of having a very clear product specification at the start of the project to avoid going off in the wrong direction. And we learned to stay focused on products that we can market as well as design. Some lessons learned have since been ignored from time to time but always reinforced as the result of expected negative consequences.

However, it was only through trying and being willing to fail that we progressed. We didn't get the first wireless right, but we persisted for four years until we did, and it has been our most successful product ever. We didn't get bark control right the first couple of tries, but in time and with the determination to keep coming up to the plate to try again, we developed the best line of bark products in the world, and the category outsells all others in number of units sold annually. Remote training is now a significant part of our business and continues to grow as we constantly improve it. The only way we are sure to fail is by failing to try. With persistence and determination, with a willingness to accept mistakes, and the intelligence to learn from them, we will ultimately succeed. And we are not alone. Every great company that I have studied is full of many failures early on, and the key that made them great in the long term was their persistence.

ADDITIONAL FINANCING

To meet our continued growth, we were constantly in pursuit of more investors. It seemed every other day wearing our best suits, we were trying to impress some new venture capital firm, investor, or banker. We talked to a lot of people, struck out nine times out of ten, but had enough hits to get the sufficient financing to carry us through.

Some of the key new investors were Tom Wylie, Jimmy Smith, and Rich Ray. Tom Wylie was an investment banker for J.C. Bradford. He was in charge of finding companies to take public, and his personal investment was a huge vote of confidence and was something we could brag about to others. Tom was also an excellent advisor on the subject of going public. In 1997 when we decided to take the plunge, Tom's firm was selected to be our lead bank on the IPO.

Jimmy Smith was the retired chairman of First American Bank, the second largest bank in the state of Tennessee. Jimmy was introduced to us by way of Otto Wheeley, and his investment was one that spoke well of our company. Jimmy also was a great help in introducing Jim and me to First American. They replaced our Third National Bank loan with a much larger line of credit that year.

Rich Ray also invested that year and was coaxed into joining our board. Rich had recently retired as CFO of Clayton Homes, a billion dollar manufactured-housing company located in Knoxville. Rich had been involved in taking Clayton Homes public, and during his tenure had raised over $1 billion in public funds. His experience and insight on the public financing arena has been a great asset ever since.

THE YEAR IN SUMMARY

From reading our history and particularly the new product development experiences in 1994, one could conclude that we failed a lot. It's true. However, the key to long-term success is not batting 1,000; it's not getting everything right. Success is having a good idea, knowing where you want to go, not fearing to fail, learning from what doesn't work, and being persistent and determined until you get it right.

We failed in many ways with the initial Radio Fence, but by 1994 we had it right. There was still room to improve, but we had an industry-leading technology that met the customer's expectations. Other categories, such as bark and remote training, had a long way to go. But a characteristic of Radio Systems then and now is never being afraid to try and to keep after it until we succeed. I hope and trust that this will be a characteristic we honor and encourage for generations to come.

Most importantly, as a result of our new improved product, our bold pricing, and to some extent the mistakes of our competitors, we accomplished what we set out to do. We defended the integrity of the category and our market share. In spite of still-ferocious competition, we even gained share. We finished the year having doubled revenues to over $15 million ($25 million) and increased unit sales from 30,000 per year to over 120,000! As a result, after only three and a half years in business, we overtook even our largest rival, Invisible Fence.

We were now #1!

CHAPER 8

FROM CRISIS TO LEADERSHIP

In retrospect, the mistakes we made at the beginning of 1995 seem obvious. However, in our defense, one would need to understand our perspective going into that year. We had just experienced growth in 1992, 1993, and 1994 of 50, 60, and 90% percent, respectively. Thus, our analysis and forecasts projecting another 50% increase looked reasonable, if not even conservative. A substantial amount of the forecasted sales was to come from new products, particularly the new Wireless Radio Fence for which tools were complete and parts to build were in stock. The engineer just had "two weeks worth of tweaks" to do. We were only a four-year-old company with little new product development experience and were very confident, as it turned out overly confident, of our ability to introduce new products on time and within specification.

With another record increase in sales a certainty, the big challenge for Radio Systems Corporation, as advised by our board of directors, the bank, and others, was to build "depth of management." It was a surety that with our success and growth, we would need to do an IPO in the near future. To do so would require Jim Hudson, our CFO, and myself to be absent from the everyday running of the business, so we needed a strong team behind us that could be dependable. It all sounded very reasonable. It wasn't.

A few things did not turn out as planned. First, due to years of not being able to get timely supply, our customers had stocked up when given the opportunity in late 1994. Thus, they were all very heavily inventoried going into 1995. Not only was the increase in 1994 partially a result of "pipeline fill," many of our customers did not need much product for the early part of the coming year. Second, most of the new products did not materialize, which I will describe in more depth a little later. Simultaneously, "depth of management" turned out to be a euphemism for burgeoning overhead. In sum, operating costs were sky rocketing, sales were flat, and new products were either behind schedule or failed altogether and had to be scrapped. We were in for a difficult year.

NEW PRODUCT DEVELOPMENT LESSONS

It is funny now to look back at the catalog that we introduced in January of 1995. It included the introduction of our first SportDog remote trainer with a five-mile range for under $99 ($163/2018). We also were introducing our new voice recognition bark collar that memorized a dog's unique bark using a voice chip, and the big item, our new Wireless Radio Fence that used radio frequency technology to set boundaries.

For years our customers had asked us to develop a sporting dog remote trainer. They assumed that our products were similar enough to Tri-tronics and that we could do for that category what we had done for the containment category. However, we didn't have the long-distance RF expertise required in-house. I had shared our need with Dennis Poole, our account manager with Whitways, one of our two primary contract manufacturers in China. Dennis said that such a product would be easy, that he could have the design contracted out, and Whitways could produce it for a price of around $30. This conversation and quote happened early in 1994. During the year, we would get regular updates that progress was being made, but there was always a glitch or two, and we would be continuously told that samples would be forthcoming soon.

By the end of 1994, we were being promised that we were just a month or two away from production. Catalogs promoting the product went out in January, and hundreds were pre-sold to our customers. Our competition was nervous and amazed at our promised price and performance. We then began to get reports that the small glitches, in fact, were very serious problems, the biggest ones being that we weren't getting anywhere close to the promised RF range or cost. Finally by late spring, Whitways informed us that they simply couldn't make the product at all. Needless to say, this went down poorly with many of our customers. Thus, we ignobly ended our first foray into the sporting dog business.

The voice recognition bark collar was a very clever, patented concept we invented. We contracted with an outside inventor/engineer to help us with the design and development. The idea was that a consumer would hold the collar near their dog, press the record button, and the dog would then be coaxed into barking. With the dog's unique sound pattern recorded, the bark collar would only correct the dog with its bark, eliminating the false activations that other products on the market experienced. It also had a microprocessor that provided up to ten levels of correction.

We spent two years trying to perfect this product but to no avail; returns were well over 50% throughout its life. One problem was keeping the microphones clean and reliable. Further, consumers just had a hard time getting dogs to bark into the microphone. The instructions were complicated, and the usability was simply not good nor consumer friendly.

Both of these failures paled in comparison to the Wireless Fence fiasco. The idea behind the product came from a conversation with one of our sales reps in Chicago. He and I were driving to Sears to make a sales call when he asked why we couldn't have the receiver only go off when we lost the signal rather than when we detected it. Then, we could create an area covered by this signal and avoid burying wires. I quickly explained to him that this would be impossible because the receiver would always be on, and we would drain batteries within hours. However, on my return, our product engineer and I discussed it, and he thought that with certain techniques, it could be done. We just needed someone to design the RF portion for us.

We had hired a purported RF (radio frequency) engineering expert to work for us to develop this project. The engineer could only work part-time. I seem to recall just about 20 to 30 hours a week at most. (The other half of his time was spent renovating a family barn. We were constantly competing with the barn project for his time.) His idea was to send a radio signal from a central unit at 27 megahertz, similar to the same frequency in handheld remotes. His objective was to get a range of up 300'. This he was able to do, and by August of 1994, we had our tooling done and complete product assemblies ready for final testing.

Unfortunately, the final testing was problematic. Everything worked except for a small matter of keeping the range constant. If we set the range at 250', for example, the weather, passing obstructions, the position of the dog, etc. could cause the range to change dramatically from the target to as little as 50' to the maximum 300'. This required just a small "tweak," and the engineer began saying in August that he was just "two weeks" from completion. From then until February of 1995, every time I asked him about our progress, he would look me in the eye and say, *"I just need two more weeks."* If you ever see me smile today when someone tells me anything will take "two weeks," you will know why.

By February of 1995, it was clear that the Wireless Fence could never hold a boundary tolerance; the fundamental concept of using high frequency RF was flawed. The engineer was brought in specifically for this project and it had failed, so I had to let him go. However even on that day, he insisted that the product was good; it just didn't meet all the specifications!

We have as our first company value, *"Try a lot of stuff and keep what works. Mistakes are part of the learning and growing process."* While this is all well and good, we leave out the fact that mistakes can be incredibly painful and expensive. However, through mistakes we are supposed to learn. Through the mistakes above, we have learned many valuable lessons.

First, contracting design with outside contractors requires intensive project management and involvement. Simply providing a specification and hoping for a final product that meets it on time is a fanciful wish. We learned from this first lesson and have since developed some expertise in managing development programs with outside partners.

Second, we learned to be persistent. We spent 1995 with egg on our face in the sporting dog world and continued to be a joke until 2003. But we never gave up and kept trying. By 2007, our SportDog brand was number one in the industry and selling over $18 million ($22 million/2018) annually. Likewise, our first bark collar was a failure. It would have been easy to have just given up after two years of poor sales and incredibly high returns. We could have simply accepted that we were just a pet containment company. Instead, we continued to turn out generation after generation of designs until we began to introduce models that were clearly the best in the industry. By 2007, we would sell over 500,000 units a year with likely something over 90% market share in the category.

This persistence paid off with the wireless fence more so than with anything in our company's history. It would have been quite easy to give up on the concept after the original design failure. What we set out to do had never been done before, and one could easily rationalize that it must then be impossible. Yet, we kept pursuing our product concept. We ultimately contracted with Concord Microsystems, and they spent three years and over $1 million ($1.2 million/2018) of our money but developed a product that really worked. We introduced that product in 1998, and it quickly revolutionized the containment category and our company. By 2007, that single product was 34% of all containment sales, 38% of all containment profits, and by far the most successful product in Radio Systems' history.

LEARNING THE VALUE OF EMPOWERMENT
THE BEGINNING OF "PROFIT TEAMS"

While I have learned and borrowed many ideas from others, either from reading, listening, or observing, I can honestly say we learned about empowerment on our own. Sure, everyone has been talking about empowerment for years, but we stumbled across it out of necessity. If it wasn't for empowering associates to take control and make decisions, we simply would not be in business today.

At the end of 1995, we had our one and only sales decline, a modest 2.3% but still far below our 100% increase estimate. As a result of our expense planning, according to that estimate, we lost $1.3 million ($2.1 million/2018). Jim Hudson, our CFO, and I huddled for days in a conference room pouring over general ledger accounts wondering what we could cut. In the end, we concluded we were just too detached from many of the company's expenses to wisely make decisions. Thus, we had a company meeting with all 60 or so employees and said simply, "Team, we cannot figure this out ourselves. Either we all work together and turn our business around, or none of us will have jobs by the end of next year." A little motivation is always helpful!

So, we created what we termed then as "Profit Teams." Each team consisted of associates from various departments and was given a set of general ledger accounts. For example, there was a team focused on office expense that looked at everything from copiers to office supplies. Of course, there were people on the team who worked in the office, had traditionally bought these supplies, and used them. However, there were also associates from quality, the warehouse, assembly, and other departments. The great thing about these other associates was that they questioned everything. If the best explanation someone had for why we were doing something a certain way was *"We have always done it that way.",* it raised a red flag.

While there were many costs that were reduced through smarter purchasing, the biggest savings came in the elimination or reduction of processes. Countless activities were being performed that brought little-to-no-value to the company and were eliminated.

As a result, our company experienced the single biggest turnaround in our history. We went from a company that had flat sales of roughly $13.5 million ($21.8 million/2018) and losing $1.3 ($2.1 million/2018) in 1995 to a company that grew by 44% to $19 million ($31 million/2018) and made $2 million ($3.3 million/2018) in profit, a $3.3 million ($5.4 million/2018) turnaround! It is true that we did have some favorable events happen in the marketplace. Two of our bigger competitors failed that year. However, the single most important contributor to success was the creation of our profit teams and how they both turned around our bottom line and became an integral, fundamental part of our culture. They later became known as continuous improvement teams, but their importance remains.

We are convinced that the team members who are the front line know our business better than anyone else, and it is our philosophy to empower those on the front line to make as many decisions as possible. Empowerment is not a just a good idea that we read in a book; it is quite simply why we are in business today.

COMPETITION

K9 Corral. One of our most fierce competitors was K9 Corral as described in an earlier chapter. They began retailing pet containment kits for $79 ($130/2018) at Target while our cost of goods was over $80 ($132/2018). They forced us to China, and they forced us to the ASIC technology. As a result, we eventually forced them to call it quits. With our matching outsourcing and low cost, we were able to come close to their price. However, with our superior quality, we began winning battles against them. More importantly, their lack of quality and after-the-sale service put them out of business. Their owner was looking for a simple product he could broker and was not prepared for all the headaches that come with building a business in this category. By 1996, his company ceased to exist.

No More Fence. Similarly, Waters Research, which made the No More Fence brand, also had incredibly high product returns and had no infrastructure to service them. They had three marquee accounts – Handyman, a home center chain headquartered in Chicago with over 100 home centers, Sears, and PetSmart. I had talks with their owner in January of 1996. I remember I was somewhat impressed and curious when he drove up in a bright red Porsche in front of a very expensive Italian restaurant on Chicago's Michigan Avenue where he asked me to meet him. I was less impressed when he stuck me for a $100 ($161/2018) lunch bill (remember this was back in the day when I could travel on $50 ($80/2018) for food all week). The owner had a new product that he was excited about, something called a "Littermaid" that scooped cat waste automatically.

He had just bought the rights to market it. We spent several months discussing a possible acquisition, but in the end, we took the chance that we could win PetSmart, 80% of his sales, without buying his company. Fortunately, we did win PetSmart that spring. We won the PetSmart account by being aggressive. We offered to buy out the No More Fence inventory at the stores and warranty their product, giving customers our product in place of the faulty No More Fence product when they called with a problem. It was aggressive, but it's how we won what is now our largest customer.

BUILDING OUR BOARD OF DIRECTORS

Another positive outcome from 1995 was adding Don Johnstone to our board of directors. All of our directors have provided invaluable, priceless guidance over the years, but Don would be one who I would consider my best CEO-mentor. His intelligence and insights have guided me so many times in so many ways, it is hard to imagine our company having anywhere near the success it has had without him.

I found Don by reading about him in the newspaper! He was the CEO of North American Phillips/Magnavox for 11 years and was responsible for relocating them to Knoxville nearer their factory and call center in East Tennessee. Don took the Magnavox brand from $800 million in revenue and an operating loss to a very profitable $2 billion enterprise. He claimed, and I have no reason to doubt him, that he was the longest tenured CEO in the television-manufacturing business due to the high pressure and thus high turnover in that industry. Prior to Magnavox, Don was CEO of Litton Industries, and prior to that he worked at GE, where he reported directly to Jack Welch. A Harvard graduate, Don is smart and has the ability to cut to the root of an issue with laser-like precision.

I have so many quotes and anecdotes that I have taken from Don that I could dedicate a whole chapter to the subject. Instead, I'll just share a few.

"The cost of complexity is immeasurable." This gem shared by Don adorned our walls in poster form for years, and if they have not yet reappeared, they likely will. Don's advice speaks directly to one of our four principle operating strategies, "Efficiency through simplicity." The fact is that complexity creates a tremendous burden on an organization, and the costs created by complexity are in fact immeasurable. Thus, we heed Don's advice and constantly strive to drive for simplicity. We do this through numerous informal and formal processes, including business process improvement (BPI), etc. The problem with complexity is that it is like a fungus; you

think you have reduced or eliminated it, but in very short order it reappears. Fighting complexity is a never-ending battle but one that must be fought.

"You cannot control your sales; the market will do that. You cannot control your margins; the competition will do that. The only thing you can completely control is your costs. So, control your #!@ costs!"* This timeless quote has been repeated by me hundreds of times. Don fought and succeeded in the very tough television-manufacturing business, and his quote is likely even more true in that industry than in our situation, but it is nonetheless words of wisdom for any company.

"You have to operate every day; you have to strategize every day." Don cautioned that too often executives go off to some exotic retreat for a few days or a week and plan strategy. Like war, plans need to change continuously as the events in the field change. One can't plan strategy once a year or so and expect it to work. It is a living, breathing, ever-evolving plan to achieve one's objectives.

"One hundred percent of the money we spent on advertising was wasted." I believe I was something of an advertising cynic long before Don shared his experiences, but he definitely reaffirmed my conviction. Don would tell me that at Magnavox they would spend $50 million a year in advertising, but he was convinced that it was all wasted and didn't directly sell a single television. So why would he do it then? He bought advertising to tell his retailers that there was a big promotion, so they in turn would load-up with product and give his brand advantageous display space which then sold the product, not the advertising. I'm sure the "100%" was said more for effect.

"What's correct? What you told the press or the financial information you mailed me?" The first time I met Don for lunch, this was his first question. I had not done many media interviews at that point, and so in one with the newspaper just before meeting Don, I was a little more aspirational than factual. Don had the newspaper article and financials I had sent him. He wisely pointed out how important it is not to get too exuberant in interviews, stay conservative, or don't say anything at all. If we were to go public and someone bought our stock based on the wrong expectations, we could end

up in a lawsuit. I've always remembered my first meeting with Don, his first question, and his advice.

Another board member that joined us at the start of 1996 was Doug Grindstaff, Sr., father of our future VP of marketing and new market development. Doug was introduced to us by Otto Wheeley as so many others were. Doug had recently retired from serving as president of Genesco Shoes, one of the nation's largest shoe manufacturers headquartered in Nashville. Prior to that, he had spent over 20 years with Proctor and Gamble, last serving as president of P&G – Canada.

Doug first invested in Radio Systems Corporation in 1995, and almost immediately we began to fall below expectations. Luckily, Doug is now able to laugh about those early days when he was afraid he had made a really bad investment.

At first, Doug did some consulting for us for additional stock options. I can't remember the return he claimed we would make on the investment in his consulting, but I remember it was very high. The good news for both of us was that what he delivered and exceeded his claims. Doug joined our board in January of 2006.

CREATING THE PETSAFE BRAND NAME

Arguably one of the most significant actions we ever took and one that definitely contributed to our big turnaround in 1996 came from a suggestion by Doug Grindstaff. Up to that point, we had had only one brand, Radio Systems, and one flagship product name, Radio Fence. Doug rightly argued that the problem with one brand was that it couldn't simultaneously be our premium flagship brand and at the same time be the low cost "fighting" brand. For years we tried to sell our single brand to everyone, from Kmart and Walmart to Petco and Home Depot. The problem with that strategy was that each retailer liked to take a different margin. As a result, some retailers, such as PetSmart, refused to carry our product because it was the same as what Kmart was selling. Others, such as Petco, that did carry our product anyway were continuously upset with us because of the promotions that Kmart would run.

While we were at the rebranding business, we also realized that "Radio Systems Corporation" was not a great brand name for pet products. We hired an ad agency in Chicago by the name of Schafer, Carter, Condon (SCC), and began work on creating new brand names. We gathered ideas from our associates, those at the agency, and Doug suggested the name "Guardian."

Where did PetSafe come from? In the fall of 1993, we agreed to let David Rogers, who lived in Burford, England and Nick Tollemache, his close friend who was also English but living and working in Hollywood, California to be our exclusive distributors for Europe. At dinner one evening around the table at David's house, David's wife, Sarah, was tossing out ideas for the name of her husband's new company and eventually suggested "PetSafe." David and Nick liked it and called their company PetSafe, Ltd. When our ad agency asked for suggestions, I threw in the name PetSafe because I had always been fond of it.

The agency spent several thousand dollars researching and testing various name options. In every poll, PetSafe always came in first and Guardian second. Thus, we made our selections. PetSafe would be our flagship brand, and Guardian would be our lower cost brand to sell to the mass merchants. I later would joke with Sarah that I spent thousands researching names when just a dinner with her would have been sufficient.

We also realized we needed another brand for the home centers, positioned between the specialty pet trade and the discounters. Not wanting to create a third brand, we divided the PetSafe brand into two series, a Premium Series and a Select Series. At the beginning, all the product was the same, just with different packaging. Over time as new products came out, they would be first launched as a Premium product and the older product would cycle down to Select and then eventually on to Guardian.

These new brands were introduced in 1996 and significantly impacted our business. One of the most measurable successes was the winning of the PetSmart business. We were fortunate that their current supplier had terrible quality issues, but having a pet specialty exclusive brand was key to beating out the others also vying for their business.

FINANCING

In addition to Doug Grindstaff's investment in 1995, Otto Wheeley also introduced us to Michael Mars, whose family owned the M&M/Mars companies, one of the wealthiest families in the U.S. and owners of one of the largest privately-held companies in the world. Michael was in training, traveling the world doing different jobs within the family company. We were fortunate to meet him while he was working as a second-shift supervisor in the M&M factory in Cleveland, Tennessee (the world's largest M&M factory).

In addition to Michael's investment, he provided significant advice and assistance. He was a passionate marketer, understood brand building, and of course was very familiar with the pet industry (Mars owns Pedigree and KalKan, among other pet brands, and is the world's largest pet food maker). Michael was kind enough to introduce me to Pedigree managers in England, Japan, Thailand, and other countries, and they provided invaluable guidance as we entered those markets.

Michael stayed an active investor for many years, and finally upon his retirement from Mars in 2006, he agreed to join the RSC Board.

Through 1995 and 1996, we were constantly meeting with investors, private equity firms, and individual investors. In total, we raised around $800,000 ($1.2 million/2018) with the biggest amount coming from the Tennessee Innovation Center (TIC), a venture fund set up by Lockheed Martin. This venture fund was a requirement as part of their contract to manage Oak Ridge National Laboratories.

SUMMARY

We began 1995 full of youthful but naïve optimism. We plummeted to near bankruptcy, but through the perseverance and talents of our associates, we emerged as the clear leaders in our industry. Our value of "try a lot of stuff and keep what works" was on display every day. We made a ton of mistakes but learned from each one. At the end of 1996, we had revenues of $19 million ($30 million/2018), over twice that of Invisible Fence, our largest competitor. The fierce low-cost imports were in retreat; all but one would be out of business within a year. We had fought many battles and came out victorious. Along the way, we attracted tremendous new talent both on our board and as associates, talent that would contribute dramatically to our success in the years to come.

A FATHER'S SON

CHAPTER 9

PETSAFE LEAPS FORWARD

(Summary provided by Chris Chandler, Petsafe's CFO)

In 1998 we launched the Petsafe® Brand and made the first "big" acquisition which was a pet door company. The background there is that the salesman at a competitor's, Lance Tracy, was continually beating us in the market, so we hired him to work for us and start the SportDOG® Brand. This allowed us to enter the market for hunters, which was a big goal of ours.

Eight years later, in 2006 we had another watershed event as we acquired Invisible Technologies, Inc., which owned the Innotek (Petsafe's biggest competitor at retail) and Invisible Fence brands. The company that launched us into the pet containment business was now under the Radio Systems' umbrella.

Just two years later, in early October 2008 we were on track for a record year and our VP of sales, Willie Wallace, told me we had this year in the bag. However, just a few weeks later the recession began to take hold. Several banks failed, fear gripped the industry, and orders virtually stopped.

By December of that year, it was time for a new strategy. We called in all our managers and told them we suspected this recession could be unlike anything the company had ever seen. Before the meeting was over, we had come up with a theme that the rest of the company could understand and had identified areas that we could pull back on. The "Bubba Gump" strategy was born as we wanted to make sure our ship would weather the storm. Survive we did, and 2009 set us up for some unprecedented acquisitions as other owners had become nervous to continue.

In February 2010, we acquired Premier Pet, which diversified our portfolio into toys and non-electronic, behavior products. We followed this acquisition with Vet Ventures, Inc., which had the Drinkwell pet fountains. We also acquired JGB Distributing, which was the largest Invisible Fence distributor.

Our growth continued as we made a big splash into the cat market in 2012 with the acquisition of Lucky Litter® , which had the ScoopFree automatic litter box.

Then in 2014, we made a cultural shift, from a product-focused design company to a customer-focused innovation company. This started with one of our board members, Glenn Novotny, inspecting one of our new products in a board meeting that had generated excitement with the SportDOG® team. Glenn sat back and said,"This is a cool product, but have you ever thought you should love thy customer and not love thy product?" He left it at that, and our COO, Willie Wallace, couldn't get what Glenn had said off his mind. *Love thy customer* was born!

By 2017, we approached $500 million in sales, with over 720 teammates around the world.

Note: *Chris Chandler has been with Radio Systems since 2004, serving as CFO during this time, and has been instrumental in all stages of growth.*

THE DEVELOPING OF
AN ENTREPRENEUR

(Summary provided by Willie Wallace, CEO – Petsafe)

The evolution of Radio Systems over its 27 years (at the time of this writing) is indeed remarkable and certainly the result of a great team working together. It was, however, primed by the entrepreneurial spirit of Randy inherited from his father, Tom. I met both Tom and Randy in 1995 as a sales agent. As a very happy owner of the Radio Fence, I was eager to meet them both. I visited Knoxville to learn about the products of Fi-Shock and Radio Systems and quickly realized that the Boyds were all about action and vision. After working with Randy for the last 23 years, I would say my initial assessment was true.

For almost five years, I represented Tom and Randy's companies in the Western region of the country. The two were very similar in their unbridled optimism, energy, and bias for action. You could almost see their minds turning with a great new idea or approach. I consider Tom the ultimate entrepreneur and have often said that if you looked up the word entrepreneur in the dictionary, you would see his picture. What I've always seen remarkable about Randy is a clear vision of where the business needs to go coupled with the best listening skills I've ever witnessed. I can't count the number of times when Randy would come to the senior team with an idea that I might consider a little crazy or a bit too bold. However, after I had a chance to marinate on his idea for a day or two, I would realize it just might work. It was these ideas that pushed our business forward. Our first value is "Try a lot of things and keep what works." It's not for a nice looking passage to be posted on a wall; we've lived it!

As I have worked with a number of entrepreneurs over the years, mostly from firms we have acquired, I've learned one of the most unique characteristics of Randy is that he was able to make that leap from entrepreneur to a strong and solid CEO and chairman. He was able to accomplish this by listening to and trusting his team and delegating decisions and judgments to the experts throughout the organization. Simply put, he is an exceptionally strong leader. That leadership will serve him and those he leads for years to come.

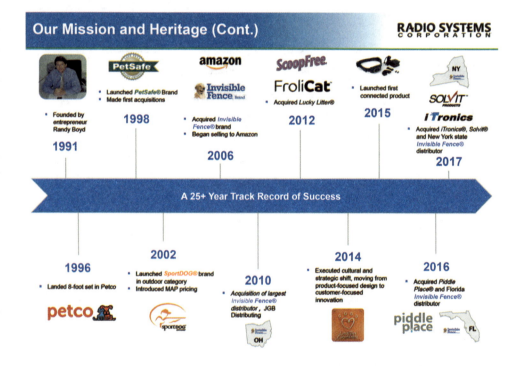

Our Mission and Heritage (Cont.)

RADIO SYSTEMS CORPORATION

- Founded by entrepreneur Randy Boyd
1991

PetSafe
- Launched *PetSafe®* Brand
- Made first acquisitions
1998

amazon
Invisible Fence® Brand
- Acquired *Invisible Fence®* brand
- Began selling to Amazon
2006

ScoopFree
FroliCat
- Acquired Lucky Litter®
2012

- Launched first connected product
2015

NY
SOLVIT PRODUCTS
iTronics
- Acquired *iTronics®, Solvit®* and New York state *Invisible Fence®* distributor
2017

A 25+ Year Track Record of Success

1996
- Landed 8-foot set in Petco

petco

2002
- Launched *SportDOG®* brand in outdoor category
- Introduced MAP pricing

SportDOG

2010
- Acquisition of largest *Invisible Fence®* distributor, JGB Distributing
OH

2014
- Executed cultural and strategic shift, moving from product-focused design to customer-focused innovation

2016
- Acquired *Piddle Place®* and Florida *Invisible Fence®* distributor

piddle place
FL

SECTION III

FAMILY BRINGS BALANCE

CHAPTER 10

JENNY JOINS THE FAMILY

Randy met Jenny Houbler, the love of his life in 1984, and they were married on March 2, 1985. He gained a beautiful, smart wife, and I gained an extraordinary daughter-in-law. I don't want to claim any extrasensory perceptions, but I knew the first time I met her that she would be Randy's lifelong mate.

Jenny was an adopted child. Her father was in the Army based in Germany when he and his wife adopted Jenny. She could not have been adopted by a better couple.

They made me wait three years to give me a grandson, but he and his brother were worth the wait. Thomas was born June 8, 1988, and Harrison was born July 5, 1993.

Jenny is an accomplished musician and loves to play Scottish, Irish, and Bluegrass music using a fiddle, banjo, and mandolin. She studied in Scotland with a famous fiddle instructor. She fell in love with the Scottish pubs where people would gather to play their instruments and socialize, so much so that she decided to open her own Scottish pub in Knoxville, Tennessee. She named it the "Boyd's Jig & Reel," so the local people would have a place to play her favorite types of music.

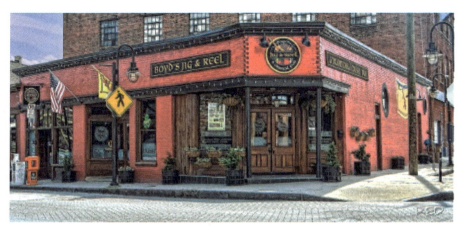

*Randy's and Jenny's sons, Thomas and Harrison,
following in Granddad's footsteps.*

A FATHER'S SON

SECTION IV

PAYING THE RENT
GIVING BACK TO THE PEOPLE
OF TENNESSEE

In the foreword, I pointed out that Randy's motto is a quote from Harry D. Strunk – "Service is the rent we pay for the space we occupy."

Randy had done extremely well in business but recognized that just making money wasn't all there was in life. He made his money the hard way and wanted to do things that would improve the lives of the people around him.

Randy has donated generously to many charities across the State of Tennessee. He has focused mostly in the area of education, sports, and entrepreneurial companies.

He does not give frivolously, rather, he looks at each and every charity and analyzes what they will return to the public. He has been instrumental in bringing new exhibits to Zoo Knoxville, and he has greatly helped the Heritage Center in Townsend and various sports facilities at the University of Tennessee. Many schools have enjoyed his support with tablets, libraries, and buildings for classrooms. He supports the Boy Scouts of America, Big Brothers Big Sisters, the Great Smoky Mountains, United Way, the Knoxville Symphony, and many others.

He continues to search for new charitable areas where he can make a difference. His dedication to helping others is best expressed through comments by those who he has helped.

CHAPTER 11

TIME TO GIVE BACK

Randy loved his time in the Boy Scouts. He always quotes the Boy Scout's motto: *Be prepared*. I believe this motto had a lot of meaning to him as I have never known him to go into a meeting without thoroughly preparing himself nor into any other venture that he would enter.

He follows the Boy Scout Law. *A Scout is Trustworthy, Loyal, Helpful, Friendly, Courteous, Kind, Obedient, Cheerful, Thrifty, Brave, Clean, and Reverent.*

Most importantly I have never known him to tell a lie.

Randy – A Tried And True Boy Scout.

STARTING KNOX ACHIEVES

Randy has always been passionate about education, a strong interest he shared with Mike Ragsdale, who was the county mayor for Knox County, Tennessee. Mike recounts a telephone call he received from Randy.

"Randy called one day and said, "Let's get together, we haven't seen each other in a while. Why don't you come out to the house and have breakfast one morning?" So, I said, "Sounds great."

I had something on my mind, which was college access for Knox County children. He had something on his mind, which was to make Knoxville and Knox County the most pet-friendly city in America. Randy gave me a really good pitch on why we should make the community very pet-friendly, and it was an exceedingly good idea. I bought into it and said, "I'll do anything to help."

I think at that point in time Randy thought, "Okay, we'll probably wrap up this meeting," and I said, "I've got something I want to mention to you. There are too many of our Knox County school children who graduate from high school and aren't taking advantage of their talents. I'd like to put something in place where they go to community college for free, and I need your help in making it happen."

It was very interesting because I saw the look on his face. He lit up with a smile. We talked about lots of things that were happening to kids when they didn't go to school and get an advanced education, and I knew right then he had bought into it completely. We started talking about how we'd put it together, how we'd make it work, and truly, within a couple of weeks, Randy had a board pulled together of some distinguished community leaders, most notably Tim Williams and Rich Ray.

We went down the hall and got this guy who was the city mayor at the time; some people have probably heard of him; his name was Bill Haslam. We really started Knox Achieves at that point in time, but Randy was the guy who was instrumental in making it happen. He was passionate about it; he wanted to make it work and did a great job, not only in recruiting the board members but raising the dollars to make it happen, and he did it in an incredibly short period of time."

Randy recognized that this program should be expanded statewide and possibly nationwide. From this platform he accepted a voluntary job with the state to broaden this program.

The following chapters are a summary of Randy's commitment to the state of Tennessee in his own words.

CHAPTER 12

THE DRIVE TO 55 – TENNESSEE PROMISE

In 2012 at the Republican Convention in Tampa, Governor Haslam came to speak at a lunch with the Tennessee delegation at our hotel one day and asked if he and I could meet privately afterwards. He explained that while he was proud of the successes his administration was having in K through 12 education, he felt not enough progress was being made in higher education. Because of my work with tnAchieves, he asked that I join his administration in an official position. After some discussion and reflection, I declined but did offer to lead a small task force for 90 days to do some research and make a proposal. He accepted this compromise.

Later at the convention, there was another lunch in which I sat by Senator Alexander and explained what I had just volunteered to do and asked his advice. He gave what turned out to be great counsel! Everyone will suggest you reorganize, he said, but if you do that, the governor will spend the next four years just doing that. It will be very contentious and controversial, but reorganizing by itself won't move the needle. Focus on improving outcomes first and organization second, he suggested. We heeded his advice with great results!

The governor suggested a small team for me to work with: Bill Lyons, his former senior policy advisor at the City of Knoxville and a UT professor of political history, and Emily Barton, a senior member of the Department of Education who was doing work on college readiness. Together we embarked on an intense statewide listening tour, interviewing dozens of thought leaders in higher education. I even traveled to Boston to meet with their secretary of education, Paul Reveille. We also met regularly to brainstorm policies and ideas, and in December we presented our report to him. There were many recommendations, including one that suggested that the state find a way to cover the scholarships for tnAchieves statewide.

During this process I learned two things. First, while it was interesting to write the report, there was far too much left to learn than three people could do part time in just 90 days, and without someone there to execute and see them through, little would likely happen. Second, this was the first time I had been away from my company for any extended period. While still CEO, I spent 90% of my time on the project. I discovered, to no surprise, that the incredibly talented, empowered leadership team did just fine without me being there day-to-day. As a result, I offered to take the entire year off to serve as the special advisor on higher education, a new title we made up.

I've joked often that, while I am usually pretty humble, in this particular case, I may have been the only person in the state who met the two key requirements the governor had for this position. The first was that the person had to work for a year completely free of charge. Second, they had to be totally unencumbered with knowledge of the subject. I knew nothing and would work for free, so I got the job! The truth was there weren't a lot of people trying to elbow me out for the position!

There were some key advantages I had coming into the position. While "totally unencumbered with knowledge of the subject" might be a little overstated, I did have the advantage of coming in with fresh eyes and asking hundreds of "dumb" questions about why we were doing things a certain way. Often the best answer was "because we always have," or "it would be too hard to change." The other advantage was that I didn't have a "turf." Everyone recognized that I was temporary, had no department to champion for additional power, and didn't have an agenda. I could be disruptive but in a non-threatening way. In addition, the governor had my back. Everyone assumed, and I never tried to dissuade them otherwise, that I spoke for the governor's office, so when I called a meeting, for example, everyone came.

From all the interviews, there were literally hundreds of good ideas shared. However, as I knew from business, the key to success is to differentiate the great ideas from the good ideas. The definition of the great idea is the one that moves you faster and further toward your mission. The problem I discovered in higher education was that there was not a single overarching mission.

A mission should be both aspiring and inspiring. A great mission lives in the space between the probable and the impossible. If you can just do what you would normally do every day and hit your mission, your target is just the probable and not very inspiring. However, if you have a mission that is so aspirational that no one believes it is possible, then it is ignored.

One fateful morning I was having breakfast with Rich Rhoda, the executive director of the Tennessee Higher Education Commission (THEC), who had served in different roles in higher education in Tennessee for nearly 30 years. I was lamenting the fact that we didn't have an overreaching mission to target. He corrected me by saying that in fact, yes, we had a mission, and it was published in the "Public Agenda," a report produced every five years. In the 2010 version, there was a mission that by 2025, 42% of our population would have some type of postsecondary certificate or degree. I was so excited!

"That's great, we have a mission!" I exclaimed. "And how did we come up with that mission?" I asked. "Well, if we keep on our current path, we will go from 32% to 39% by 2025." "Yes, but why 42%?" I asked, and Rich replied, "Well, that is what we estimate will be the national average then."

"Wait, our inspiring, state educational mission is by the year 2025 to be average?" "Yes," Rich replied, "Our goal is to be average in 12 years!" I couldn't imagine any situation where "average" would be anyone's goal. If a new UT football coach was hired and stated his goal in 10 years was to be average in the SEC, he would be immediately fired, but in education, far more critical to our state than football (though I know some will disagree with this statement), our state was willing to settle for average.

Then I asked, "Based on the same forecasts and experts, where do we need to be?" It turned out that everyone from Georgetown to the Gates Foundation to the Lumina Foundation forecasted that by the year 2025, 55%

of our state's workforce would need to have some postsecondary certificate or degree. For every percentage we fell short, that was a percentage of our population that would be unemployed or underemployed.

It was clear we had no choice. Hitting the 55% was not nice to have but a must have. I discussed this with the governor, and he agreed. I sent weekly summaries to him early every Sunday morning, and this week I sent him one with the idea of branding our target "The Drive to 55." He responded back that he liked it, and later that month included the brand and the launch of the initiative in his State of the State Address in 2013. Thus, the Drive to 55 was born.

CHAPTER 13

SPECIAL ADVISOR ON HIGHER EDUCATION

The governor gave me the choice of working out of the capitol or the offices of THEC, and we agreed that since most of the policy experts were at THEC, I would set up shop there on the 19th floor of Parkway Towers on James Robertson Parkway.

I retained the title of CEO of Radio Systems for myself but asked Willie Wallace, my COO, to run the day-to-day operations. In a memo to my team, I noted that if I had truly done my job, then I would have created something bigger and better than any one person and that it could continue to grow and prosper, focused on our mission, led by great people executing sound strategies, and all within our set of values. I had absolutely no doubt that I had total and complete confidence in the team. They didn't let me down! Often people would say during that year that while I was not getting paid, my biggest sacrifice was all the opportunity costs I was missing by not running my company. The truth was that the company did better without me than with me!

My usual week was to drive to Nashville early Monday morning, be on a conference call with the senior staff for their weekly Monday morning briefing, and then start my work week in Nashville. I would be there usually Monday through Thursday staying at a hotel downtown. I'd try to find some projects to do at UT and around the Knoxville area on Fridays. UT was kind enough to give me a meeting room in the main library as an office (students were puzzled to see the stream of visitors coming for meetings in this little study room).

Rich Rhoda was a great partner and gracious host. One of his kindest gifts was allowing one of his associates, Mike Krause, to work with me in addition to his normal job of reviewing accreditation for programs at the institutions. He was an eager, intelligent, and innovative resource with a great can-do attitude. Mike went on to become director of the Drive to 55 when I left, and then later the executive director of THEC.

Also on the team were Will Cromer, the governor's senior policy advisor, and Jayme Place, his education policy advisor. While both had many other responsibilities, I think they were really passionate about the Drive to 55 project and were huge contributors to our research and policy development. The governor recommended I meet Drew Kim, a former policy advisor under governor Bredesen, and we immediately hit it off. I personally hired Drew as a consultant to provide additional thought leadership, organization, and research. Lastly, Anne Buckle, a Harvard graduate in education who had been working in the Customer Focused Government department, allowed me to recruit her as my only full-time staff person. Between us, we were the Drive to 55 core team, though key players from other departments, especially the THEC team, were regular parties to discussions and analysis. Of particular note were Russ Deaton, Jessica Gibson, and Rich Rhoda at THEC, and later Emily House, who did great work on statistical research and analysis.

By July, we had the basics of the five key strategies we recommended the state pursue to achieve the Drive to 55. In colloquial terms, they were to get them ready, get them in, get them out, finish what you started, and accountability and alignment.

We developed a large binder full of detailed briefs on each strategy with a range of initiatives, but it started with a call to action as follows:

Governor Haslam has challenged our state with the Drive to 55, which is both inspirational and aspirational. Not only is it a mission for "K to J" education with the J standing for jobs, but it is also a mission for workforce development. It is a mission for economic growth. It is a mission to reduce unemployment and incarceration while improving health and quality of life.

The Drive to 55 is the mission of Tennessee. The Drive to 55 is our challenge to increase Tennessee's postsecondary attainment from 32.1% today to 55% by the year 2025 for adults from ages 25 to 64. But this metric is not just about four-year degrees and higher. It is about degrees and certificates from community colleges and technical colleges in fields like welding and mechatronics. This mission measures our workforce readiness, and every national study concludes that by the year 2025, 55% of Tennesseans must have a certificate or higher to meet workplace demands. Every percentage below 55% represents our fellow Tennesseans – our children – who will be unemployed or underemployed. This mission is not a hope it is a necessity.

The great news is that we can achieve our mission. It does not require a breakthrough in science or technology but is rather a question of political will. We simply have to commit to this effort, trusting that we can do it.

The Drive to 55 Initiatives (D55I) follow. They include strategies to help Tennessee youth have a strong start by dramatically reducing remedial math, increasing college readiness, and increasing dual enrollment. They include strategies to make Tennessee the first state in history to promise every high school graduate an opportunity to get a degree or certificate free from direct costs and with mentor support. They include strategies to leverage amazing new technologies to increase access, improve quality, and reduce costs of higher education. And they include more opportunity for the 940,000 Tennesseans with some college but no degree to finish their degree and improve their potential for a better life.

In September we had a big launch event at Nashville's new convention center. We wanted video from employers, students, and parents; we wanted stickers, shirts, coffee mugs, and other promotional material; we wanted a great logo and brand and great innovative and inspiring speakers. It would take too long to go through the state procurement processes, so I donated the money to pay for all of it, including flying down a couple of great speakers. First, we had an expert from Georgetown University to speak on the coming crisis in skilled workforce shortage. Second, we flew down Anant Agarwahl from MIT, who was pioneering a new online education concept called a

MOOC or "Massive Online Open Course," through a joint venture between Harvard and MIT called EdX. Between the videos, these two speakers, the governor, and I, we had a very high-impact launch. In fact, I had several attendees share afterwards that there had never been such a big production so well done for a launch of an initiative in state government before. Over 100 educators and legislators from around the state attended.

The launch was my opportunity to reinforce the importance of the Drive to 55 and to share the key five strategies that we would be implementing to reach our goal. While we shared the problem and the general strategy, we didn't share the exact solutions. Following are the five strategies along with the actual solutions we later recommended and eventually passed.

It is important to know what the Drive to 55 is. It's a big number. To go from 32% to 55% would require an additional 494,000 certificates and degrees. It is not just four-year degrees. It includes one-year certificates earned in welding for example, at our Tennessee Colleges of Applied Technology and associate's degrees at our community colleges. In fact, forecasts showed that 60% of the certificates and degrees needed would come from one of these types of schools. It's not just any degree but very specific degrees. Using the University of Tennessee's Center for Business and Economic Research (CBER), we were able to forecast what skills were going to be undersupplied and which ones we would be oversupplied. For example, we were on track to have 400 too few accountants but 12,000 too many psychology majors.

Strategy 1: GET READY

Unfortunately, too many high school graduates were getting a diploma that didn't prepare them for college. In fact, 80% entering community colleges had to take either a remedial math or English course. If they did, then they had only a 5% chance of graduating. When you consider that these students are entering college paying tuition for a class that feels exactly like high school, because it is, and then getting no credit for it, it is understandable why so many would drop out so quickly.

We had a few key proposals for solving this. First, using a program called Seamless Aligned Integrated Learning Support or SAILS, students in high school could take an online class in a "flipped" classroom, where the teachers served as tutors when students needed them, but the lectures, workbooks, and tests were online. This program was pioneered by Chattanooga State and led by Kim McCormick. In its first year, 80% of the 500 students who took the program passed all math requirements to enter college and thus would not need remediation. As I have found often, the best solutions don't need to be invented; they just need to be found, and often they can be found right here in Tennessee. The key was finding the great ideas and then scaling them.

We also recognized the value of dual enrollment courses, where students could take a college course in high school and get credit for it. House education committee chairman Harry Brooks was a big advocate of dual enrollment and dual credit, and we consulted with him often. If a student took and passed two dual enrollment courses, there was a 95% chance they would go to college. However, only about 8% of high school students did so. One problem was the cost. The Tennessee Education Lottery Scholarship (TELS) set aside money to pay for 50% of the $300 to $400 cost of a course up to four courses. Some were arguing for it to be applied to more courses, but we argued "it's better to have some for all than all for some," meaning we wanted everyone to have at least one or two classes rather than a few to be able to take four to eight. Thus, we suggested changing the formula so that every student in high school could take at least two courses free of charge.

Strategy 2: GET IN

Once we had them ready to enter, we needed to insure they could successfully enroll. As with SAILS, we already had a model that worked. With tnAchieves, we had a proven template that began small in Knox County and by the fall of 2013 was in 27 counties offering scholarships to 51% of all high school graduates and sent over 5,000 students to college that year free of charge and all matched with a mentor to guide them. When doing the financial modeling, we had six years worth of data with a sample size of 50% of the state, so there wasn't much guess work in forecasting costs. And as mentioned in the chapter on tnAchieves, it was efficient and effective; students not only entered college but were 50% more likely to stay once they got there.

When reviewing our list of initiatives on a menu of options I kept on a spreadsheet with the governor during the summer of 2013, I remember him circling the "Tennessee Promise," the working name I gave to the idea, and he said "This is the One," meaning of all ideas on the page, he thought this was the one that was the biggest game changer.

Like nearly everything I've experienced in business and public service, having the idea is the easy part. Next would come how we were going to pay for it. We spent the second half of the year debating options, starting with 12 then whittling them down to seven then three then two and finally the one that we proposed.

We were very fortunate and had an asset that very few other states had. The lottery scholarship had been in place since 2004. Originally, the law required a $50 million reserve, but a few years later as the reserve grew, legislation was passed to raise it to $100 million. In 2013, it was over $430 million! By transferring the excess to a new trust fund to guarantee the Tennessee Promise scholarships, we protected the funds from future non-education raids but also set up an endowment that could make our promise one that we could honor for generations! In addition, each year the lottery continued to generate more funds than Hope scholarships required, so the additional surplus each year would also be transferred into the Tennessee Promise endowment. The interest on this endowment would contribute to the cost of the program.

But that alone was not enough. Since the beginning of knoxAchieves, it annoyed me that the authors of this program undervalued and discouraged technical and community colleges. If a student chose the more expensive choice, a four-year university, they would get a Hope scholarship of $4,000 per year. However, if they chose the lesser expensive option, a community college, they only got $2,000 per year. If they chose a technical college, they only got $1,000 per year! The more frugal they were, the more they were penalized.

If the logic behind the way it was structured was to reduce the cost of high-achieving, wealthy students, it may have been successful. However, as a tool to increase access and help the state achieve the Drive to 55, it was a colossal failure. In 2004, Tennessee's college going rate was 61%, and Alabama's was 59%. Alabama did not create a lottery scholarship in that year, but Tennessee did. Ten years later, Tennessee had awarded $1 billion in scholarships. Our college-going rate declined from 61% to 59%. Meanwhile, Alabama's increased from 59% to 62%! If our goal was to increase college-going rates and thereby increase degrees, we obviously needed to change course.

Another interesting stat we discovered was that 40% of those winning the Hope scholarship had family incomes of over $100,000 per year. In other words, they were going anyway. Importantly, as I will explain in a moment, 40% of Hope scholarship winners didn't maintain their GPA and lost the scholarship within the first year.

The second critical change was to make the awards fairer. Our proposal was to give all students $3,000 per year for the first two years, and for four-year students, $5,000 per year their last two years. Thus, they would still get the same $16,000 if they stayed. By doing this, not only was it fair, but due to the fact that so many lost their scholarship so quickly, the state saved millions on not giving the higher amount to four-year students that first year, only to see them lose it by the second year.

I learned quickly that just because an idea is logical, that doesn't mean it is easy to execute. First, there was fear of "Touching Hope." I had literally dozens of educational professionals and political insiders lecture me on how difficult the Lottery and Hope was originally to pass, and "Whatever you do, don't open that can of worms." Even in the 11th hour, there were serious debates among myself and the governor's team about whether this was a battle we wanted to fight. "This is why we came here, to fight the hard battles that really make a difference," I would argue. Governor Haslam is a great leader, who encourages discussion and debate on issues and then makes reasoned and thoughtful decisions with the collaboration and support of his team. In the end, after we agreed on a course of action, everyone came together as a team and fully focused on getting it done.

The governor announced the Tennessee Promise at the State of the state in 2014. I remember multiple conversations with then senate minority leader Kyle, who had lectured me on using the excess lottery funds for some useful purpose, and my listening politely and knowing that was exactly what we hoped to do. Before heading into the State of the State, I went up to him and said "We listened to you. I hope you like what you are about to hear." When the governor announced the Tennessee Promise that every high school graduate could now go to technical or community college free of charge in perpetuity and with not a single new tax payer dollar, Senator Kyle was the first to bolt to his feet to cheer. Everyone followed suit. This truly had bipartisan support.

The State of the State was on a Monday, as it usually is, and my last day was on that Friday. I had promised the governor one year, and I had stayed a year and one month. My last four days were eerily quiet. All the proposals were made, the research was done, the position papers and FAQs written. Now it was up to the governor's highly competent and determined legislative team to get it passed. I am a minimalist, and my office was pretty sparse, excepting a couple of white boards and poster boards, my personal lap top, which I packed up, and a few files that I handed off to Anne. I said my goodbyes to all the new friends I had made. Maybe like friends made in wartime or other crises, you build a strong and lasting bond. Regardless of how often we would see each other in the future, we would always have a strong bond of friendship, knowing that we had done something very special together. But Tennessee Promise did not go smoothly in the legislature.

In 2013, I was part of the first Leadership Tennessee class, and one of my classmates was Claude Presnell, who had already become one of my best friends in my new role as special advisor. Claude was the president of TICUA, the Tennessee Independent Colleges and Universities Association that represented 33e private non-profit colleges from schools as small as Johnson University to Vanderbilt. I had the goal of visiting each campus, and while I only made about 25 of them, Claude traveled with me to each one from Memphis to Jefferson City and all campuses in between.

The problem that all four-year universities had was that they were worried that with only $3,000 for the first two years, students wouldn't be able to afford the first year. There could be no evidence of this, but they were concerned. As the advocate for TICUA schools, Claude led a very aggressive campaign against our proposal. I had left Nashville, but he and I saw each other every month in Leadership Tennessee. The organizers of Leadership Tennessee even thought it would be good for the two of us to debate the issue one day in class, which we did. While both of us held very strong views, we managed to keep the conflict civil and remained good friends during and after. In the end, as often happens, we reached a compromise. Rather than $3,000 the first two years and $5,000 the last two years, we changed it to $3,500 and $4,500, while keeping the $3,000 per year for the community colleges. This had the effect of reducing our estimated savings on first year Hope drop-outs by half, but our model still showed positive cash flow.

When it came time for a vote, we won 31 of 32 Senate votes, and 91 of 98 House votes.

The governor asked me before we announced the Drive to 55 what I thought our biggest challenge to accomplishing our goal was. I then answered immediately something that I still believe is true. There is no financial and technical barrier preventing us from hitting our goal. Our biggest challenge is our culture, a culture of low expectations. Too many of us too often don't believe a better education and a better life is possible for our children and ourselves. With the Tennessee Promise, this changes. Now every kindergartner and their parents can know that a college certificate or degree is part of their destiny; they can dream big and expect a better life. All they have to do is start preparing themselves. That is the hope, and that is the way we accomplish the Drive to 55 and our state's destiny.

Strategy 3: GET OUT

Once we get students in, we need to get them out (i.e. graduate them). Unfortunately, like other states, too many fail to graduate. In 2013, only 59% of students that enter a four-year university graduate in six years. At our two-year community colleges, only 26% graduate. Some schools, like Southwest Community College in Memphis, had an 8% graduation rate after six years. However, like in so many cases, a solution was right in front of us and in our state. The TCAT's (Tennessee College of Applied Technology) were graduating 84% of their students in one year, on time and even more importantly, 92% of them immediately went into a job for which they were trained.

The key initiatives proposed to tackle this were more modest but important. There was a program called Degree Compass that was invented by Dr. Tristan Denley, who at that time served at Austin Peay University. This software program allowed students to map out their course of study for a particular degree, and based on their ACT and high school and college grades that they had made so far, it would predict what grades they would make in the courses they had left. Thus, a freshman could see far in advance if he or she was going to have difficulty in a future class.

The Tennessee Board of Regents, led at that time by chancellor John Morgan, also was experimenting with "block scheduling," which basically meant following the TCAT model of sending a cohort of students through a degreed program together and eliminating choice along the way. Just giving students a plan to follow along with a group of peers turns out to be extremely effective, increasing retention rates by as much as 50%. We also advocated for more funding to expand this program.

In the end, only Degree Compass got additional funding. There are many things left to do on the Drive to 55, and this is one of the most critical programs. To bring more attention to this, in 2016, I, along with a handful of others, such as Barbara Hyde from the Hyde Foundation and Krissy DeAlejandro from tnAchieves, founded Complete Tennessee, a new non-profit to shine a spotlight on the issue by annual accountability reports, provision of leadership training for community college leaders, and support and research for new innovative solutions.

Strategy 4: FINISH WHAT YOU START

In Tennessee about 60% or 40,000 of our annual 60,000 high school graduates go on to pursue some type of post-secondary certificate or degree. The math in 2013 had changed a little since, but it still highlights a critical point. If 100% of the 20,000 who didn't go decided to go, and 100% of those actually graduated, 12 years times 20,000 would give us an additional 240,000 certificates or degrees. Remember, earlier I mentioned we needed 494,000 to get to our goal of 55%. Thus, there simply aren't enough traditional students for us to reach 55%. It is impossible without adults returning.

One bright point was that about 940,000 Tennesseans had some college but no degree. Reaching out to them was a great opportunity. The biggest challenge for adults is often not just the financial barriers but the time barriers. For most, they already have a current job, family, and many other obligations so that there is very little time to go to classes. We have to meet them where they are. Offering more evening and weekend courses and having more online options is key.

The major initiative we advocated for was more funding for online programs; however, rather than each school creating their own, the original idea was for UT and TBR (Tennessee Board of Regents) to work together to create courses that every institution in the state could share. It may make sense for six public universities to offer engineering courses in classrooms for geographic convenience. However, it makes no sense for each university to create their own online courses when they can share them.

Strategy 5: ACCOUNTABILITY AND ALIGNMENT

Lastly, the fifth strategy was around accountability and alignment. Everything we would do in the first four strategies would be a colossal waste of time and money if we were educating people in areas in which there were no jobs. Too often counselors would give students an aptitude and preference test suggesting what they were good at and what they would like, and the intersection of these two points would be what was recommended that they pursue. However, there is a third critical leg to the stool, and what can you get a job in!

Senator Mark Norris proposed and passed a new bill in 2013 called LEAP or Labor and Education Alignment Program. Like most bills, it suggested vaguely that labor and education should work closely together and that ECD (Early Childhood Development) should prepare a report once a year highlighting progress and showing where the jobs were and where more training was needed. However, there wasn't a blueprint on how to do that. So we put together a broad team consisting of Labor, Department of Education, Higher Education, Senator Norris' office, ECD, and TBR to create a plan. The Brookings Institute is heavily involved in workforce training issues and also consulted with us.

After six months with lots of discussion, research, and leadership from Ginger Hauser with TBR and the Brookings Institute, a proposal was put forward. First, we would create a workforce subcabinet that would consist of all departments involved in aligning workforce and education. Rather than just ask them to get together to have discussions, we gave it a job. We proposed that the governor offer a competitive grant to communities to first identify skills gaps in their areas, then create and propose a program to fill those gaps. The winners would be chosen by the workforce subcabinet, and we originally asked for $10 million.

One of the not-so-secret motivators was to incentivize the local collaboration. To be eligible to compete, the local community had to have a committee that represented K through 12, higher education, local government, and business to identify these gaps. While the measurable benefit was winning the grant, we believed the even more important benefit was to increase collaboration. We also proposed small facilitation grants.

In the end, the governor supported all but the facilitation grants, the legislature passed the funding, the workforce subcabinet was created, and LEAP actually had real teeth to get things done. In my view, the money spent on LEAP grants is some of the most effective dollars we spend in all of education.

The accountability part of this strategy focused on better reporting of how our higher education institutions were doing. We wanted to make sure students were good customers of education with easy access to graduation rates, job placement rates, average incomes per degree by university, and other critical information. This was something that needed little funding and that THEC was eventually able to do.

SUSTAINING DRIVE TO 55

The Drive to 55 wasn't a one-year idea or initiative, but instead, the mission of the state for the next decade. It can't be a fad but must be the singular disciplined focus of our state. It helps us define the good from the great ideas and is critical to insure Tennessee's economic success. While much has been done, there is still much left to do. Increasing physical access to TCATs needs addressing as do more convenient options for adults. While high school graduates are more prepared than ever for career and college, far too many are still woefully unprepared. Graduation rates are just barely inching up, but far too slowly. Fixing the leaky pipes is critical and urgent.

My year in 2013 working on the Drive to 55 was a pivotal moment in my life. When I complained government work wasn't for me when the governor first recruited me, he said, "Everything you say is true. Things will take three times longer, and you'll have ten times as many stakeholders to convince. But if you can get something done, it can be transformative and far bigger and more permanent than anything you can ever do as a business person or philanthropist." By creating the Drive to 55, the Tennessee Promise, SAILS, LEAP, and so much more, he proved what he said was true.

I'll always be thankful for the incredible experience during 2013 and serving as the governor's special advisor on higher education. I'm thankful to the governor for the opportunity and to all of the friends that I made and collaborated with to accomplish some truly great things.

CHAPTER 14

TN COMMISSIONER OF BUSINESS DEVELOPMENT

Randy was appointed as commissioner of business development by Governor Bill Haslam in 2015 and served two years until resigning in 2017 to run for governor.

During his time of service, he brought in 50,000 new, high-paying jobs and an additional $11 billion in new investments. This broke all previous records.

Randy and the governor made several business trips to Japan, Korea, and one to Israel. The Israel trip was very informative and inspiring for Randy. He had the opportunity to meet with their former prime minister, Shimon Peres. He still talks about Mr. Peres' statement on living. In their meeting someone asked what contributed his long life and all of his successes. He said, "You are old when you can count more accomplishments of the past than dreams of the future. You are forever young when you can count more dreams of the future than accomplishments of the past."

Randy loved his job and the ability to serve the state. He paid his own expenses and took no salary. His boss, the governor, always joked about having a guy work for him at no pay.

One of the most important lessons he learned in this job was that for Tennessee to be competitive with other states and bring in higher paying jobs, our education system had to reflect our needs for skilled employees. To do that we had to change our direction on a state level to graduate these types of future employees. He had begun the process before taking this job by establishing Tennessee Promise. He knew that more was required, and it would take a governor dedicated to expanding the programs already started to reach the goals we needed to obtain.

To do this, he felt that he could only accomplish this on the scale needed as governor. He announced his decision in 2017 to run.

SECTION V

THE LURE OF ADVENTURE
SEEKING THE CHALLENGES

THE FOLLOWING STORIES ABOUT
RANDY'S VARIOUS ADVENTURES WERE
WRITTEN BY RANDY.

These adventures were to be read by his family only.
Because they present a fuller picture of Randy and what drives him, I asked
for permission to share his adventures with the readers of this book.

CHAPTER 15

CLIMBING MT. RAINIER
PUTTING MYSELF TO THE TEST

I called the Summit Haus, the recommended supply and rental store on the property at Rainier Mountaineering, Inc. (RMI), about two months before our climb to check on some equipment. The woman I talked to had a few problems with my questions and confessed she was really a guide just helping out in the store. I hadn't had the opportunity to talk to a guide directly before and began to ask her questions. It was a slow day at the store, and she indulged me for about 30 minutes. Most of my questions were around conditioning, and after describing what I was doing, she said, "Oh, I think you'll do fine. You will suffer, of course, but you will do fine."

The words "You will suffer, of course" played back in my mind over and over again from then until I was halfway back down the mountain before I understood what she meant. It's simply one of those challenges you have to experience to appreciate, but to aid my slowly deteriorating memory and in the slight chance anyone else would care to know more details about my excursion, I am writing this short narrative.

Dick Bowers, former ambassador to Bolivia and hiker of the entire Appalachian Trail who recently summited Mt. McKinley, inspired me with his adventures. The writer, David Brill, accompanied him to Mt. McKinley. David subsequently wrote a book, *Desire and Ice*, about their adventure. It was an enjoyable book, providing the novices' perspective to first attempts at mountain climbing. Dick and David, with about ten others, trained for one week with RMI on Mt. Rainier which they summited.

I had always been fascinated with mountaineering, but most of what I had read or watched was about K2 or Everest, very unlikely quests for me personally. After reading Brill's book, however, I decided that I would sample the experience on something safer and more convenient (not to mention less expensive), Mt. Rainier. I contacted RMI and got the details on a trip. Over the Christmas holidays, I discussed the trip with my two brothers-in-law, Jim Anfang and Thomas Evans. Both wanted to go too, and so the three of us signed up in January for a May 23 to 25 attempt. For those curious about costs, the fee for this program was $751 in 2003 when I made the trip, but that excludes airfare and the even more expensive gear.

Immediately, Thomas and I began a schedule of hiking mountains in the Smokies. We started by climbing Mt. LeConte in January via the Alum Cave Trail, which at that time was covered in ice and snow. We averaged a hike every other week for the first three months and every week the last month, most from 12 to 18 miles. We climbed Mt. LeConte seven times and Mt. Cammerer among others. During the week, I averaged five workouts with at least an hour of cardio, usually on the CrossRamp, StairMaster, or stationary bike. I supplemented these with weights on average four days a week. The most important part of all this was the support, or at least the tolerance, I received from my family. I was, more often than not, tired at the end of the day from the very early morning workouts and then gone nearly all day at least one of the two weekend days. Jenny and the boys allowed me this luxury at their expense.

Thomas and I arrived in Seattle on Thursday, May 22nd, met Jim, took in a Seattle Mariners baseball game, then drove to Ashford, Washington, the last "town" before one enters the Mt. Rainier Park. We arrived about 6:00 p.m., giving us another hour to pick up our rental gear or gear we had purchased. We stayed at the Whittaker bunkhouse with the other "clients", as the guides referred to the other climbers. The bunkhouse, RMI, and the Summit Haus were all clustered conveniently together in one small complex. The hotel was clean, and we shared a four-bed room, but there were no amenities such as TV or telephone (and no cell coverage in the area either). There was a computer in the lobby of the bunkhouse with an Internet connection, which made for a convenient place to check the weather forecasts.

DAY ONE

The first day of the three-day program is school, and we had ours on Friday, May 23rd. It starts with an introduction by the guide, a brief equipment check, and then a 45-minute bus ride up to Paradise, which is really a parking lot at the base of the mountain and an old, under construction, guide-service building. Once there, we put on our gaiters (protective leg coverings), our packs, and headed up the mountain for only about 15 minutes or so. There was deep snow immediately at the parking lot, so we didn't have to hike far to find an area to train. However, later in the season, schools attendees may have to hike an hour or more to get to the snow line.

We had a large group in the program, a total of 16 clients. There were two brothers from Texas, Mike and Trey, and their cousin from Oregon, Dee. There was another group of three from Houston – Tiffany, Chuck, and Sean. There were four military commando types that tended to stay to themselves, though were stereotypically loud and gung-ho. There was also a father from Washington, Lynn, who was a marathon runner, and his daughter, Lindsay, a student attending the University of Arizona in Tucson, who had previously climbed eight other peaks. One man, Steve, from Ohio came alone. He had lived many years in Guatemala, where he had climbed several volcanoes. Our party of three rounded out the group.

For school we had two instructors, John Lucio and Gale Wulff. John was the senior of the two, having guided for seven years. He was a tall, athletic early-thirty-something with a very laid-back California demeanor. He told us often that he normally didn't teach and seemed very disinterested in the process. Gale was younger, more personable, and seemed more enthusiastic. Both, however, instilled confidence in that they seemed in command of the skills needed and had more than the necessary experience.

In school we practiced a few of the basic techniques we would need for climbing over the next two days. We practiced putting on crampons and walking in them. We put on rope harnesses and practiced traversing up and down a steep hill. Most excitingly, we practiced our ice axe arrest. This is where you are expected to stop yourself and possibly the others on your rope team while falling down. In principle, you are to shift the axe that has one sharp point on the end of the handle and one on each end of the blade from your side up to and across your chest and then fall on it, all while wearing a heavy pack and falling down a steep mountain. It was easier than I expected, but then practicing for it calmly and expectedly is probably much different than it would be when really required. Later, my rope team would need to use this skill twice during our descent.

The first day was short, educational, and not physically taxing. The worst part of the day was the unexpected sun. Though only 55 degrees, it was sunny, and in spite of repeated lathering of sunscreen, nearly all got bad sun burns from the reflection of the snow. We were back in base camp at Ashford by 3:30, giving more time for last minute gear checks and then off for dinner and packing.

Thomas, Randy and Jim.

Being from Wisconsin and having climbed other 14,000' peaks in Colorado, my brother-in-law Jim underestimated the weather and gear needed. There is something peculiarly colder about Rainier than those other mountains, and being unprotected on the side of a mountain for 12 hours in high winds is a colder experience that even the most toughened Packers fans would consider difficult. Jim didn't pack a parka, and I think he will concur that he underestimated the challenge.

Packing was a challenge itself and one we had to do repeatedly. Mentally we had decided that we really didn't have to carry that much, but none of us had actually tried to put everything in our pack yet, primarily because we were picking a lot of it up in Ashford. We were in for a surprise. The sleeping bag seemed to take up 80% of the entire pack no matter how much we tried to compress it. The down parka was also a space hog. It would be hot for the first two hours, so we wanted to pack our additional layers meaning a full layer of Capilene underwear, fleece/wind stopper top and pants, plus a layer of Gortex. Add two socks, food (two lunches, one dinner, one breakfast, and about ten snacks needed!), two 32-ounce water bottles, crampons, ice axe, head light, and ski poles (for walking in the snow up to Camp Muir). We were impressed when we finally managed to get everything in our packs, but less so when we threw them on and realized what a load we were going to have to carry five miles in deep snow up 5,000' to Camp Muir.

DAY 2

I awoke way too early at 1:00 a.m. pacific time, partially out of habit back in my time zone and partially with anxiety. Am I in shape, do I really need my parka, should I rent the guide recommended one that takes less space, are my Leki poles adequate for the snow or should I rent ski poles like everyone else, should I buy the headlight with the 4.5 volt battery or will just carrying an extra set of AAs and using the one I have be OK, etc.? With no TV and not wanting to turn on the light to awaken my roommates, I lay in bed stressing over these details. Finally around 4:30 a.m., I'm confident that everyone else is awake and when asked, turns out they've been up a little while too. We all shower and do the last touches of our packing. There is no place open in Ashford until 7:00 a.m., so we drive eight miles to the next town where we can get coffee at a convenience store and use our cell phones to call our wives. (Ashford is a bad place for those who like coffee early in the morning.) We then head back and have a nice breakfast of oatmeal (Jim and I) and pancakes (Thomas) at a tavern/restaurant a few hundred feet from RMI.

We were all to meet at 8:15 at RMI for a final gear check and to break into the groups. Thomas, Jim, and I were assigned to the Group B leaving 15 minutes after the first group. In our group there were the three from Houston (the least apparently in shape of all and ones who had the most difficulty in school the day before), and the two brothers and cousin from Texas. I was a little concerned about the draw, but there wasn't much to be done. Our guides, however, were great. We were assigned Chris Simmons, the group leader, Mike Boughton, and Mario Pignataro. Chris was about 30 years old, had just gotten back from Mt. McKinley late the night before where he had spent the last three weeks summiting it, and seemed very enthusiastic and friendly. We later found out he was also a taskmaster with no tolerance for not keeping pace. Mike was younger, a little shorter, and very stout but quieter. He had been a mogul ski champion for over a decade. He had just spent the last week on Mt. Rainier teaching the week-long expedition camp, one that prepares climbers for higher peaks elsewhere. Mario was the youngest, small, but also very personable. All had summited Rainier many times with Chris hoping to go for his 15th summit with us. While we weren't sure about our other climbers, we felt good about our guides.

We were also encouraged to hear that the team from the day before made it to the summit. They were the first of the week to have done so, and the weather looked clear and warm in Ashford, so we were hopeful.

The trip started with the 45-minute ride to Paradise, a last minute gear check, strapping on the right equipment (sun hat, lotion, ski poles, gaiters), and then we set off for Camp Muir a little after 10:00 a.m. They had a 144-inch base of snow, but it was reasonably well-packed, so we didn't sink too much along the trail up. The plan, which we stuck to diligently, was to climb one hour, take a 10 to 15 minute break, then resume.

It's different than hiking the Smokies. First, hiking in deep snow is more demanding. Second, we only trained occasionally for the heavy packs. However, they were surprisingly not as difficult as we expected the night before. The grade, though, was steadily up and up. Mt. LeConte is either a 3,000' or 4,000' gain in elevation either over 5.5 miles or 8 miles, respectively, depending on the route you take. Thus, there are a few ridges where one walks along flat ground. On Mt. Rainier, every single step is up.

Still, this day wasn't too bad. The first two hours were sunny and warm, and we all overheated. Breaks were comfortable, and we snacked and hydrated. As Chris would say repeatedly, "You have to feed the furnace; you have to drink and eat at every break, or you'll cramp or get sick." The elevation was not noticeably different, and breathing was easy.

After the second break two hours in, we noticed that the summit, which had always been obscured by clouds, was even more clouded, and the weather seemed to be moving downward. About halfway into the third hour, it got progressively colder, and we lost most of our visibility as we entered the clouds. At the next break, we put on our windstopper fleece, gloves, and hats. It was very curious how fast the weather changes with elevation.

About midway up, we ran into the summit team that had set out that morning (RMI will typically have one team attempting a summit every day). They looked exhausted and dejected. The guide chatted with ours for a moment. "This was a very strong team, but we just couldn't make it. We got within 400' of the summit and had to turn back. Too much wind. Over 60 mph. We were getting blown off and had to turn back." I remembered the stat I had read that only 44% successfully summit in May. While in August the success rate is higher, at a little over 60%, the snow is less stable, and risk of falling in a crevasse is greater. I looked disconcertedly at the weather above.

The last two hours were colder still, and in the last hour, 30 to 40 mile-per-hour winds pelted us with tiny ice particles that blew off the mountain. Thomas would comment once we entered the hut that it was the coldest he had ever been. Several noted that he would get to set a new personal record the next day! We finally reached Camp Muir about 4:00 p.m. and were instructed to leave our packs outside and just bring in our sleeping bags, dinner, and any clothes we would need for the morning.

Camp Muir is a small, rustic, wooden hut about 30' by 30'. There is one platform around the top around three sides, then two other platforms on each end under the top one. On the other sides are a bench and a counter for water with additional gear stored underneath. Helmets hang from nails in the spare spots. There is just enough room for three people to sleep lengthwise, toe or head to the center on each of the platforms. With 16 people and all of our gear, it was a cozy room.

We were informed we are to go to sleep at 5:30, so we have a very busy hour and half. First, we get a demonstration on our equipment for the next day, which includes a transponder worn as a shoulder harness in case of an avalanche, a helmet with light, and a review of our rope harness. Then we get briefed on what to expect in the morning, which will start at between 1:00 a.m. and 3:00 a.m. depending on the weather. "Hots" will be served in 15 minutes which means the guides will bring in hot water for those who want to cook. Most brought some type of freeze-dried food. After dinner, we organize our gear so we will be as ready as possible for the morning and turn in to sleep.

The wind picked up increasingly to 60 mph, and the hut seemed to shake. A small sign hanging from the door was banging very loudly, but thankfully Jim had to go to the bathroom (in the latrine outside, a very cold, icy experience that made you groan to think about when your bladder demanded attention), and on his return he took the sign down. Waking at 1:00 this morning was now a good thing and helped me to go to sleep quickly, and with the exception of one bathroom visit at 7:30, I managed to sleep until 1:00 a.m. just before the guides came in to wake us. Thomas had difficulty sleeping, which played a part in his experience the next day.

Throughout the night, however, we could all hear the wind howling, and we remembered the team from the day before. Some teams never leave Camp Muir, and the prospect of sitting in the hut until 8 or 9 a.m. and then being forced to return to Paradise was very real. In the last hour or two before we awoke (obviously no one slept that deeply), we noticed the wind dying down and optimism rose.

THE FIRST HOUR
2:45 A.M. TO 3:45 A.M., 10,200' TO 11,500'

The guides roused us at 1:15 a.m., asking Group B to stay in bed to give Group A room to prepare their gear as they were to leave first, about 15 minutes before Group B. However, we couldn't help but begin preparing ourselves. By 2:00 a.m. "hots" were served. Thomas made coffee, but most just had a cold snack and drank water. Though we had over an hour from awakening to setting off, it was very hectic and busy. In the hut, we strapped on transponders, harnesses, and helmets and did the final organizing of packs. Crampons were to be put on outside. By 2:30 a.m. Group A was out the door. At 2:45 a.m., we exited into the cold and wind. We put on crampons and then were assigned our rope teams. My team was guided by Mike. I told Thomas after training together over so many weekends, it was only right that we do this final leg together. Jim was to climb with the brothers from Texas with Mario as the guide. Chris had another two from Houston (I found out later that the lady from Houston walked to the rope and decided it just wasn't her day and returned to the hut to await our return).

Mario's team was first, followed by mine with Mike, and then Chris behind us. At 3:00 a.m. we set out all roped about 20' apart, lights on, looking eerily like a snake moving slowly up the mountain in the dark, just the crunch of snow and the howling of the wind. It was very surreal. As much as I wanted to control my breathing, my heart was pumping from the exhilaration. After almost six months of anticipation and training, the final five-hour assault was beginning.

The initial pace was steady but fast, the incline moderate but persistently upward. Within about 20 minutes, Thomas needed to take a break to catch his breath. We were quickly made to understand that this was unacceptable. We were to stop only at the designated breaks, and no interim stops were to be tolerated. Chris was behind me on the last rope team and asked who it was in front of me in an intolerant tone. After a moment, Thomas resumed the march. However, in another 10 minutes he stopped again and told Mike that he couldn't go on. The air was thinner, and despite his strength and conditioning, he was having a hard time breathing and was cramping. I'm sure his not completely giving up smoking was having its effect. Mike assembled our rope team off the trail and held a brief discussion with Chris. They radioed ahead and found out that one of the members of Group A had decided he could go no further at the first break, an area called Ingraham Glacier flats (something of a misnomer). Mike asked Thomas if he could make it another 30 minutes to

the flats, but he could not. So he removed his crampons and slid into Mike's sleeping bag, which Mike had carried just for this contingency.

At altitude, one has to really work at breathing to get enough oxygen. The pressure at this altitude is roughly half what it is at sea level, and so to compensate, one "pressure breathes", a process whereby you force a long, deep breath out. Early on this is done with every step. Toward the top it may be two breaths per step. If you forget, which is easy to do, you get dizzy and can develop a debilitating, summit-ending headache, among other things. Ironically, just the act of breathing this hard can also be very tiring.

Thirty minutes later, we met up with the other two rope teams and regrouped. Mike headed back down with John to pick up Thomas and then return to Camp Muir; I roped in with Chris' team. We took a short break for food and water. The first order of business was always to throw on the parka. No matter how warm you thought you were, once stopped, you got cold fast. I was feeling good though. At no point had I gotten winded, and my legs still felt fresh. Though I was forcing myself to pressure breathe to avoid any effects of altitude, I almost felt it was unnecessary. Best of all, the wind had died down, and the sky seemed somewhat clear – clouds below, clouds above, but the space we were in was clear. I began to feel very confident we were going to make it.

THE SECOND HOUR AND A HALF
4:00 A.M. TO 5:30 A.M., 11,200' TO 12,200'

Chris announced that this segment would be the hardest of the day, a steep hour and half climb with several crevasses to cross. Shortly, there was enough light to turn off our lights, and we entered the Ingraham Glacier, where we could see several crevasses – beautiful but at the same time scary. We had to "jump" over two on the way up. In both cases, it was just a short 12" step but along a very narrow ledge. A good gust of wind at the wrong moment would have given our guides the opportunity to demonstrate their crevasse rescue techniques. On the way up, we passed two more climbers, one of the military guys, and the father/runner. The latter seemed in good spirits saying, "It just wasn't my day." At the end of this segment, I was still feeling good, and the winds were still calm, and I was increasingly optimistic, especially in light of Chris' comment that this had been the hardest section.

THE THIRD SEGMENT
5:45 A.M. TO 6:45 A.M., 12,200' TO 13,100'

Chris lied. He said we would climb steeply for about 20 minutes, and then it would flatten out. No one later ever recalled anything resembling "flat." Within ten minutes, the wind began to pick up steadily, and the temperature dropped correspondingly. Gusts hit 40 mph, and I began to feel nauseous, which I later found out most others did too. The altitude began to have an effect, and I found myself breathing very shallowly. I forced myself to focus on rest-stepping and pressure-breathing. Though my muscles didn't seem strained and I only got winded when I made the mistake of taking a big step, fatigue began to set in just from the continuous stepping up for over three hours. The wind had an unanticipated effect, too. Not only was one required to step in an unnatural manner on a very steep slope, but also it was necessary to plant the ice axe before each step to keep from getting blown off the mountain. The gusts were consistent now and really added to the work. Within the space of an hour, confidence began to wane, and doubt about physical ability and weather conditions began to dominate. Chris announced at the break that this is the point of no return.

If you don't think you can make it, you have to stay here. All commit to finishing. I made the mistake of having a "GU" gel without enough water, which ends up causing me stomach cramps in the last hour.

THE FOURTH SEGMENT
6:55 TO 7:45 A.M., 13,100' TO 14,000'

The break was very short with barely time to put on a parka, take a couple of bites from an energy bar, force down some water, and then repack and head up. Body temperature still drops significantly in this short period. The wind seems to be increasing, and the team that had to turn around 400' from the top is on everyone's mind. I just focus on taking one step at a time. The cold is becoming a greater factor. Stomach cramps are the worst physical ailment though.

THE FIFTH AND FINAL SEGMENT TO THE SUMMIT
7:50 A.M. TO 8:30 A.M., 14,000' TO 14,410'

We stopped just long enough to put parkas on permanently. With the wind and the dropping temperature, it was extremely cold. The temperature was between 0 and 10 degrees with 40 to 50 mph winds and pelting ice. Everyone was exhausted and very unsure about our potential success. We set off, and I just focused on taking the next step, one step after another. Nausea was a real problem, and I was sure I would eventually have to stop to throw up. I had forewarned Chris, and he said we would pause briefly to allow me to do that, if necessary. He was generous that way. After about fifteen minutes, we encountered Group A heading down. The girl from Arizona stuck out her ice axe and yelled "Cheers". They had made it! We knew they only had a fifteen-minute head start. Because of our loss of climbers, they probably had made a little better time. Still, if the weather could just hold for a little longer, we now knew we would summit soon.

I always wondered why climbers seemed to move in such slow motion as they were heading for the summit. I thought why don't they just sprint on up when there is such a short distance left? I doubt I can capture it in writing but know now that it is impossible. The fatigue, altitude, and cold combine to make each step a challenge. Step. Take a deep breath. Rest. Step.

We crested the summit at 8:30 a.m. On the last section, I had decided there was no way I would be up to a photograph; it was just too cold, but at the summit, we went over the lip and down 20' or so into the crater and were somewhat protected from the wind. Jim and I congratulated each other, shook hands, and had Chris take a photo. It was too cloudy for a good view, but the crater itself was beautiful. Fatigue and stomach cramps took most of the enjoyment out of the moment.

What did I think about in those last few minutes ascending and at the summit? Pride, success, accomplishment, other mountains? No. Reaching the summit had a riveting effect, and I could only think of what was really important – my family. I did get emotional thinking about them and couldn't wait to get home to be with them.

To add to our enjoyment, Chris reminded us that we had just made it half-way; we now had to go all the way back down. And while going down was quicker, it was not necessarily easier and could be more dangerous. After ten minutes to rehydrate and snack, we began our descent.

THE DESCENT TO CAMP MUIR
8:40 A.M. TO 12:00 NOON

The descent to Camp Muir took three hours with two breaks, one after each hour. Going down a steep incline is, while easier, still challenging. One danger is tripping on the rope with your crampons, which the client behind me managed to do twice. Each time the rest of the team dropped into an ice axe arrest to prevent the team from falling and the one climber from falling further. Both turned out to be no big problem though on the second we were about 50' above a crevasse.

Back at Camp Muir we were given an hour to have lunch, drink lots of water, take off and store our helmets, rope harnesses, and helmets, and repack the gear we had left in the hut back into our pack, resuming its stuffed 40-pound load, and then get ready to head back down. We were told that we could have a few minutes to rest, but we were really too busy.

Thomas had joined with the others in the hut, and they had passed the time by resting in sleeping bags as it was too cold to do much else. The other four left with Group A for Paradise just a few minutes before we returned. Thomas was happy for us, and we assured him that he made the right decision. If one goes past where they are sure they can go, it could jeopardize the rest of the team's ability to summit. We owed him for an important assist. Like the others, it just wasn't his day this day, but there would be other chances.

THE DESCENT TO PARADISE

It just didn't seem fair. After having been up for 12 hours and climbing through challenging conditions for over nine hours, we still had another five miles and 5,000' to descend in deep snow with a 40-pound pack. And while one would think warmer weather would be welcome, it just helped to drain us further. We finally made it back to Paradise at about 4:00 p.m. to catch the bus back to Ashford. Group A was still there waiting for us, and we all congratulated each other.

FINAL THOUGHTS

One would think that there would be a big celebration with all the summiteers. While I think we would have liked to, everyone was now busy making plans to make their way home. Still, while you are roped together and succeed together, it is very much an individual achievement. There is no talking in a climb except for brief exchanges at breaks about vital things such as physical condition, equipment, etc. It's a common shared experience, but experienced individually.

So what next? I didn't think I would ever climb another mountain in those last two hours up. Once was enough. However, by the stretch from Camp Muir to Paradise, I began to think of other possibilities such as higher but less challenging mountains like those found in Latin America. Jim and I discussed the experience on the way down, and I asked if it was the hardest thing he had ever done. He annually does the Birkebeiner, a 50-mile, 3 hour cross-country ski race, and he has also run 50-miles at a stretch before. He said yes, this was by far the hardest. I had to agree that it was for me too, but noted that I was already beginning to forget what was so hard about it and that within a few days, I probably wouldn't remember at all. Now that several days have passed, I was right; I have forgotten. Writing this and reading it occasionally might help me remember. But maybe McKinley might not be so unrealistic a goal after all.

For a higher price, one could also summit in a saner manner. For instance, on day one climb to about 9,000', set up camp, and practice all the climbing skills covered in school. The next morning, climb past Camp Muir to the Ingraham Glacier at 11,000' and set up camp again. Train a little more, and most importantly, just enjoy the majesty of the view and the crevasses. The one regret I have is that we were on such a pace, there was virtually no time to actually stop and enjoy the panorama. This slow ascent also allows more time to acclimate to the elevation. On the third or fourth day, depending on weather, one only has to go a little over 3,000' to the summit and then return back only 3,000'. Such a trip would take two guides and cost about $5,000 total for two to three clients.

So "Did you have fun?" No. I've been asked this several times, and fun is just not an appropriate description. The best I can do is say it was "fulfilling." There is a feeling of accomplishment in climbing mountains – the training, the preparation, the elements of nature conspiring against you. I'm just a novice, but I don't think people climb mountains "because it's there" as you often hear, but because they are here. One achieves new heights, not physically, but it is a feeling of fulfillment that makes being here more real and more alive.

CHAPTER 16

CLIMBING PICO DE ORIZABA

February 6 through 10, 2005

We shall not cease from exploration,
And the end of all our exploring,
Will be to arrive where we started,
And know the place for the first time.

— T.S. Eliot, "Four Quartets"

I begin this account of our climb to the crater rim of Pico de Orizaba, the third highest mountain in North America, with a quote from T.S. Eliot primarily to annoy one of my fellow climbers and new friend, Doug Sheaffer. Doug hates people that moralize about things, in particular mountain climbing. He related to us a story of an interview with a British climber after having summiting some high peak in the Himalayas. When asked what his first thoughts were upon reaching the top, the climber waxed eloquently on some newfound insight into the meaning of life. Then the interviewer asked the Sherpa who accompanied him what his first thought was when he reached the summit, to which the Sherpa replied, "Must go down!"

That said, I must say that T.S. Eliot best describes a key virtue of exploration, and in this case, mountain climbing. Every challenge, every new adventure brings to me a better understanding of myself and brings me that much closer to home and family and what is most important in life. This was such an adventure.

An adventure with the wrong group of people can be misery no matter where you go or what you achieve. Likewise, the right group of people can turn any misadventure into one that is enriching. In this case, I was fortunate to have every element – misery, success, and great companions. Our guide was Michael Lindaas, a 37-year-old climber residing in Bend, Oregon and seven-year veteran with Robert Link Mountaineering. Mike has the calm, easy going persona one would hope for in a guide but is also determined, confident, optimistic, and an excellent motivator as I would find out. He gave our team confidence while making the trip fun. He averages eight international climbs per year and has climbed all over the world, including summiting Orizaba eight times. As I write, he is unmarried but was making plans to change his status soon.

The clients were myself, Steve Schuckman, and Doug Sheaffer. Steve is from Montclair, New Jersey, a former botanist and now the horticulturist at a private reserve. He has climbed many places in the U.S. including Mt. Rainier twice and taken trips to Ecuador and to Mexico. Steve shared with me his very healthy perspective on climbing – it's all about the experience, not just about the summit. The odds of summiting, depending on the mountain, are usually less than 50%. If one were depressed every time they were prevented from summiting, then they would be so a lot. To be too obsessed with the summit marginalizes the rest of a truly great experience, the beautiful scenery, and the friendships. Oh, and it can also increase the probability of death. Thank you, Steve, for sharing this perspective, one that I will do my best to adopt in mountain climbing and other endeavors. Beyond improving my philosophical well-being, Steve could identify nearly everything that grew and was definitely value-added. I am advocating that Robert Link pay Steve to take these trips in the future and advertise "Ph.D. Naturalist guide included." I'm sure it would be a valuable differentiator. Steve is married with a 17-year-old son.

Doug works for a defense contractor in Sunnyvale. At 58, he no longer does five marathons a year like he used to, but I believe he could if he chose to do so. Looking ten years younger than his age and able to outperform men half his age, Doug was well-prepared for this trip. In addition, he has made many other climbs including Ecuador, Mt. Kilimanjaro, Mt. Elbrus in Russia, and Mexico. Doug has a very pragmatic, matter-of-fact way that was fun and refreshing. He also shared many funny stories from his previous climbs, including the flag "collector" who had his team in Russia do an exhaustive search for a very specific-sized Russian flag. When finally asked how many he had in his collection, the "collector" announced "one". We subsequently became collectors of any one thing we had. Doug is single and contemplating "retiring" to his native land, Oregon.

I was the rookie with only one other summit, Mt. Rainier, and an unsuccessful trip to Bolivia (which I now look upon in a more favorable light thanks to Steve). My specialty was annoying the rest of the team with new climbing product ideas from custom-fit hiking poles to the all-purpose climbing helmet with multiple shades, two-way radio, removable headlamp, etc. The best ideas, however, I am not at liberty to disclose! I have two sons, Harrison, 11, and Thomas, 16, and a lovely, patient, and tolerant wife, Jenny.

We met Sunday night, February 6th, in Mexico City for Churassco (a type of Argentinean steak) and to get acquainted and briefed on our trip. On Monday morning, we drove four hours to Tlachichuca with a brief stop in Puebla along the way where we stopped for lunch and did some shopping. In Tlachichuca, we stayed at Senor Reyes bunkhouse located in an old soap factory, an eclectic layover for those about to climb or who had just climbed Orizaba. The owner's hospitality makes any stay special, along with all the old soap-making vats and machines that were central to each room.

Senor Reyes bunkhouse. The shower house is to the left, and the bunks are in the main building to the right and upstairs.

On Monday afternoon, we walked a half mile to a small mountain and climbed to the top, roughly a 750-foot ascent. The steepness and the cactus minefield made it a fun, exciting, though slightly bloody and painful affair. That evening we had a great meal at the bunkhouse, sorted gear (almost a never-ending vocation), and watched an IMAX movie, *Kilimanjaro*, in Senor Reyes' den.

Tuesday we headed to Orizaba. We were dropped off by the truck at around 10,000' and hiked up the next 2,000' to our camp site. The truck carried additional gear to the site, and we set up camp. The area is one of the highest, if not the highest, pine forest in the world. We had a glorious view of Orizaba. As always, as soon as the sun sets, it got very cold, and we were all in bed by 7 p.m. and tossed and turned until 8:00 a.m. the next day awaiting the sun.

The trucks were 50s-style Dodge Powerwagons
with no air but well suited for the terrain.

Camping in the pine forest at 12,000'.
It's the simple pleasures.

On Wednesday we hiked to Piedra Grande Hut, a stone structure that provides a high camp for climbers to Orizaba at 14,000'. We would spend the next two nights there (if you can count summit night as a "night"). However, this day we passed it by climbing up another 1,000' to get familiar with the trail that we would use on summit day and to work on our acclimatization.

Piedra Grande Hut had a reputation as being smelly and dirty; however, with a little house cleaning when we arrived, it was adequate.

As one would expect, the trail is mostly volcanic dust and rock. It was very steep, twisted, and turned between rocks. However, when we got to our high point for the day and had a snack and water break, it was a glorious day with clear skies, a warming sun, and incredible views. We then returned back to the hut to claim our place on the wooden planks that constituted bunks and began organizing our gear for the summit while Mike prepared dinner which consisted of quesadilla's, soup, and whatever other snacks we could rummage for in our bin of food.

Again, after a long day and thin air, our only alternative was to sit up in the cold with our headlamps. We decided to turn in early and were in our bags by 7:00 p.m.

Enjoying a beautiful day during a well-deserved rest break.

THURSDAY, THE DAY BEFORE THE SUMMIT

We woke earlier on Thursday and took a two-hour hike up to approximately 15,500' to store a cache of equipment we would need for the glacier, such as our ice axes and crampons. The first hour was the same as the day before, but the second hour was much more "bouldering", climbing up and over the very rocky terrain. Again, we enjoyed a nice break at the top before returning back to the hut.

Shortly after our return, we noticed two climbers coming down and intercepted them when they passed by the hut. They were two young men from Germany. They were complaining of severe headaches, which they said caused them to abort their summit attempt at no more than 16,000'. Steve queried them on how much water they had drunk, and they said about three quarters of a liter for the day, as if that were enough. (We averaged four liters per day, which is very important in acclimatization.) They were surprised at the effect of the altitudes, noting that they climb in the Alps all the time. However, as Mike pointed out, the highest mountain in the Alps is Mount Blanc at only 15,000', and the average peaks are around 12,000'. It was interesting to see how even somewhat experienced climbers underestimate the effect of altitude.

Late afternoon we were joined in the hut by a group of six American climbers with two guides, also brought up by Senor Reyes' trucks. They were from International Mountain Guides out of Ashford, Washington. Mike had climbed with their lead guide, Mark Tucker, and their Mexican guide was a good friend of Octavio's.

For our big pre-summit dinner, Mike prepared macaroni and cheese with extra cheese, and then we set about getting our gear ready for the last time. For those who haven't climbed before, this may sound like a lot of unnecessary fretting, but one only wants to carry the minimum, yet wants to avoid freezing, starving, dehydrating, and fumbling around in the pack in the dark, wind, and cold looking for things during the always hurried breaks.

*Enjoying our luxurious accommodations
the night before the summit.*

By 6:30 p.m. we were settled and turned in to get as much sleep as possible before the 10:45 p.m. wake-up call. Being just late afternoon, knowing you have a big challenge ahead, and knowing you have to get to sleep quickly almost guarantees that you will not. Octavio doesn't even bother to try before a climb and stayed up reading. The rest of us did our best but averaged probably two to three hours of restless sleep.

SUMMIT DAY

By 11:00 p.m. Thursday night, the hut was a hive of activity with the guides boiling hot water for us to make tea, oatmeal, or other hot food, and all nine climbers "gearing up," putting on cold weather gear, filling water bottles, strapping on harnesses, helmets, plastic boots, and gaiters. By 11:45 p.m. we were ready, threw on our packs, and headed out. The other team of climbers were to set out five minutes later.

The first hour was now familiar territory, having traveled it each of the last two days. I told myself this was just a chance to loosen up like a practice lap before a long race. My mental strategy was to break the ascent down into parts of a marathon. It was going to be nine hours up and four hours down with a 15-minute break each hour. So I imagined that each hour was equivalent to three miles of a marathon and psychologically prepared accordingly.

The first break was quick and uneventful. There was little-to-no wind, and we stayed warm. The second hour was also familiar, but try as I might to convince myself it was still just part of the warm up, I could begin to feel myself expending some real energy. The boulders seemed a bit more challenging in the dark and with a slightly heavier pack.

We reached our cache of glacier equipment by around 2:00 a.m. Here we took another 15-minute break, packed the crampons and ice axes, and set up for the next hour segment. We were roughly halfway through the volcanic rock portion of the trek before we reached the glacier.

This hour was a "ball buster," as Steve commented when we got to the next rest stop. I must admit I lost my nerve in one spot when we reached a chute with ice down the middle. We were to climb up by wedging in small cracks in the rock on either side, with pack and plastic boots, and in darkness with no sense of how big of a drop it was. Fortunately, Octavio made it to the top first and secured a rope for the rest of us to hook onto in case we slipped. Maybe I worried too much as everyone made it without incident. Nonetheless, this hour was very taxing, and I believe we all were beginning to feel tired, perhaps with the exception of our guides. My marathon analogy had quickly broken down, and I succumbed to Mike's more experienced recommendation – just think of nothing else but making the next segment. However, we soon broke 16,500', which was a personal record for me. I had planned a rebel yell at 16,000' (that's "yee-haw" for any sheltered northern readers) but decided to save my energy.

In the next segment, we climbed a little less than an hour and around 4:30 a.m. reached the base of the Jamapa Glacier. Here we strapped on our crampons, stored our poles, and donned our ice axe. Sounds simple.

However, strapping on crampons in the dark and freezing cold with a heavy parka on is very awkward, and we spent some time doing this. Frustrated cursing was heard.

I was informed the night before that if one charts temperature patterns anywhere in the world, one would find that it's the coldest in the morning just before dawn. This time coincided with our arrival on the glacier, which is by definition also cold and fully exposed to the wind. Needless to say, things began to get very chilly, and everyone added a layer, some deciding to just leave the parka on at the risk of getting too warm. (Dressing is an art. During each hour of climbing, one gets very warm, only to cool down precipitously at every break.)

The glacier was distressing. It had receded significantly in the last five years, according to our guide. The base of the glacier is now terribly serrated, making footing even more difficult than it would be anyway. The angle at this point is around 45 degrees, but there are huge ruts every couple of inches. There was virtually no snow, just hard, crunchy ice.

Mt. Rainier was steep, but at least it was a hard-packed snow and relatively easy to get your footing. This was going to be a new experience.

We formed two rope teams with Octavio and me on one, and Mike leading Steve and Doug on the other. Octavio took the lead, and we began the long march to the summit. We estimated about four hours to the top with three breaks along the way. Octavio, having been up recently, suggested we take a more northern route, one that Mike had not taken in his previous summits. This turned out to be a fortuitous recommendation.

I won't recite the details of the next four hours, partially because as I write my memory is just of one prolonged beating, but I do remember that after just the first hour, I was to the point of exhaustion. I had developed a gastrointestinal bug the day before, and it made for an extremely uncomfortable ordeal. However, only three hours from the top when I was thinking very loudly that I just didn't care this badly, Mike looked me in the eye and said, "We are too close. We are all going to make this together." That was enough motivation to encourage me on for a while longer. Just make the next segment, I told myself.

I began counting steps. Each step is very short and is accompanied by a deep pressure breath, so they don't happen fast and don't cover a lot of ground. I would count to 100 and then look up. Disappointingly, it seemed that the crater rim never got any closer. About an hour from the summit, my bowels couldn't take it anymore. I let Mike's rope team pass me, and I hung by the end of Octavio's rope and had one of the most unusual potty breaks of my life. The rope, the navigating around the climbing harness strapped around my waist and legs, the 45-degree angle, the cold, and the wind weren't really so bad, but the serrated ice seat was a little unpleasant. At least I got to take some time to enjoy the awesome view. Octavio definitely had to go over and above to bear with me through this ordeal.

However, this seemed to help, and with new found vigor, Octavio began to lead me straight up the glacier toward the rim, while the other rope team traversed more to the right. For the rest of the climb, I can only recall a lot of moaning, desperate pressure breathing, and thinking that I really just didn't care about reaching this summit that badly. Finally Octavio, probably sensing that I was faltering (it wasn't hard to do), yelled "It's your summit! Only 20 meters more." That was good enough to motivate me for another five minutes, at which point I looked up, and the rim was still the same distance. "It's your summit! Only 10 meters more." I think I managed to make him promise that this was in fact the case and continued on. One additional, pleasant surprise, though it shouldn't have been, was being met with the smell of sulfur, much like rotten eggs, that one finds at volcanoes.

Finally I stepped over the crater rim. Some might jump for joy; some just stand and revel in the view and the victory. As for me, I crumpled to the ground, curled up, and lay there for several minutes. I remember forgetting to breathe and suddenly being aware of it and forcing breaths. It's a little scary knowing that breathing doesn't come automatically, and you have to consciously work to do it. I was also aware that Octavio and I were alone there for a while. However, within a few minutes Mike, Steve, and Doug materialized.

The wind was strong, and it was cold. The inside of the crater was deep and steep, I'm told 400' down and very wide. The wind would catch the volcanic dust and rock from inside the crater and pelt it at would-be admirers. Steve took some photos, and after a brief discussion, we decided not to traverse the crater rim and instead, head down. Immediately.

As the Sherpa said, everyone's primary thought having achieved the pinnacle was not how happy we were in our accomplishment, but that we "Must go down." The object of mountain climbing isn't to get to the top but to get back to the bottom. The prospect of plunging down the steep, icy glacier wasn't appealing, but with Octavio this time trailing and swearing, I had nothing to fear. With him on the rope to prevent a fall we headed down. Amazingly, while fatigued and exhausted, the descent wasn't too bad. It probably has to do with heading into thicker air. Nonetheless, it took about four and a half hours for all of us to make it back to the hut. It's kind of like finishing a marathon and then having to walk back to the start. It's anti-climactic, annoying and numbing.

When we arrived at the hut, we found the other team of climbers already there. We had seen them ahead of us as we were heading down and joined up with them briefly a couple of times. But not until I reached the hut did I realize that they didn't summit. They had chosen the standard route, gotten within 300' of the summit, and hit a sheet of ice that they did not feel they could cross, and then had to descend. They had endured nearly everything we had but without the satisfaction of making it to the top. It made us realize just how fortunate we all were to have made it.

From here, we packed and then waited for Senor Reyes' trucks which arrived around 4:00 p.m. We all crammed into them and enjoyed a two-hour drive through the dusty, rutted roads traveling about five to ten miles per hour back to the bunkhouse. We were exhausted but fulfilled. Hot showers, semi-clean clothes, and a great meal with beer and bed by 7:00 p.m. made for a sufficient celebration.

*From left to right; Randy, Steve, Doug and Mike,
cleaned and fed the morning after and ready
to head back to Mexico City.*

Just before bed I may have made maybe my one serious mistake. I called home from the pay phone in the bunkhouse and got my wife, Jenny, on the line. I only had 35 pesos, so I only had two minutes to talk. I told her I had two pieces of good news, something I had rehearsed saying on the journey down. "First, I summited. Second, it's just too painful, and I'm retiring from mountain climbing." Then I lost my connection.

I'm told mountain climbing is like childbirth. After a few days pass, you really don't remember the pain, just the accomplishment. As I look back, it was really only the last five hours up and the first hour down that was shear hell. One can endure anything for six hours, right? However, Jenny told my Mom, and now there is an anti-climbing alliance that intends to use my own words as their principle weapon against me.

But, after all, "We shall not cease from exploration." Maybe something a little more leisurely next year, like Mt. Kilimanjaro perhaps.

Thank you Octavio and Mike for making the trip so successful and Steve and Doug for making it such an enriching, memorable experience. And, most importantly, thanks to my wife and family for allowing me to experience this and future adventures.

CHAPTER 17

CLIMBING
MT. ACONCAGUA, ARGENTINA

February 2007

View of Aconcagua from the plane.

"Time has left me with one conviction...I would define myself as a good listener of stories, especially those about to happen. I believe in stories, in measureless ambitions, and the arbitrariness of desires. Every so often, the ideas one believes in and obeys set up a hedge around life and say ... 'You can't go beyond this point.'"

— Luis Jait, psychotherapist in Mendoza, Argentina and mountaineer, from his book *Aconcagua: In Praise of Self* written after his second attempt and first successful summit of Aconcagua

"I choose stories that are about to happen. Those that humans need to be happy, to resemble their ideal self, those that are rewarded by a sensation of surprise and excitement in which
one is oneself and the other, where one is known and unknown. My time is the time of desire, of tomorrow."

— Luis Jait, *Aconcagua: In Praise of Self*

I read a book entitled *The Seven Summits* by Dick Bass and Frank Ridgeway about Dick and his friend, Frank Wells' quest to be the first to climb the highest summit on each continent. Dick successfully completed the quest in 1985 while Frank did all but Everest, giving up on that peak after three unsuccessful attempts. Their quest inspired me to imitate them, though likely only doing six of the seven, skipping Everest.

Dick is the founder of Snowbird ski resort in Utah and still regales clients with his stories. Frank was president of Universal Studios and later became famous as the president of Disney under Michael Eisner and is given credit for much of the early turnaround and success there. He died in 1990 in a helicopter crash while on a ski trip. If you are interested in a real mountaineering adventure, I would recommend their book.

Anyone reading this knows me and knows how this story ends, so you probably already know that I have decided not to pursue the Six Summits. Dick and Frank quit their jobs, left their families, and dedicated their lives to their quest for three years. By doing it first and 20 years ago, many of their challenges were much harder than they are today, such as organizing the logistics of climbing Mt. Vinson in Antarctica or getting permission to climb Mt. Everest. Still, it is not a quest taken lightly. I soon realized at Aconcagua (and was reminded that I had learned this same lesson already in Bolivia) that I really don't like long expeditions where one spends many weeks freezing at breakfast and dinner, 12 to 16 hours a day in a sleeping bag to stay warm, the stench resulting from no showers by anyone in the camp for weeks, the unsanitary toilets, and the constant battle with the symptoms of altitude such as headaches, dehydration, and diarrhea. In the end, I realized that to accomplish some of the highest summits required expeditions and to accomplish them, they have to become more than just a once a year week-long endurance test to stay in shape and see the outdoors; they need to be an all-consuming passion. In some activities passion is an option and defines how well one does, but in mountain climbing, it is a cost of entry, a prerequisite. My problem with this mountain was mostly mental; I just wasn't passionate enough about attaining its summit.

Further, I had promised Jenny (and myself amongst others) that I would not put myself in too much jeopardy. We had particularly cold and windy weather with a forecast of another storm to come. Two weeks before our trip, one of my guides was with another client on Aconcagua and saw someone get picked up and thrown 15' through the air, luckily at a spot where he wasn't blown off the mountain. I met a young Englishman being evacuated by helicopter to save his frostbitten toes. The risk-to-reward ratio was simply not appropriate, at least for me.

So why write a diary about this trip? When I didn't summit Huayana Potosi in Bolivia, I didn't write anything about it. However, I now regret it. As I look back on that trip, it was possibly the most memorable. Thus, I want to capture my thoughts now about Aconcagua as a reference for myself to share with any that are curious about the place and the experiences I had there and to recommend some aspect of the trip to anyone healthy enough to do a little trekking. There are many who visit the park not to climb but just to take in the scenery, which is truly awe-inspiring. I hope you find the following interesting and that it inspires you to create a story about your future visit to that part of the world.

SATURDAY, FEBRUARY 4TH

There are only overnight flights to Santiago similar to Europe, so one leaves at 10:00 at night and arrives around 9:00 a.m. the next morning, losing two hours (it is two hours ahead). After a quick but trouble-free transfer, I boarded a LAN airlines flight to Mendoza, Argentina and arrived there at 11:30 a.m. Colon Falconi, my guide from Ecuador the previous year, met me after clearing customs along with Edison Ona. Colon is 32, single, a part time architect, and has been a mountain guide for 15 years. He has started his own guiding company but is just now fully committing himself to it.

Edison has been Colon's friend for 18 years, is 36, also unmarried, and has been guiding since he was seventeen. His English is perfect; not as much can be said of Colon's. Of the two, Edison is the most experienced, and he also has his own guide service, which he takes very seriously. In spring of the year before, he attempted Mt. Everest from the Tibetan side but pulled out 1,000' before the summit.

We were met by a "Campo Base" (pronounced boss-ee) driver and also Andrew Turton, who arrived on the plane with me from Brighton in the U.K., who had contracted with Campo Base too. We assumed we were just sharing a bus ride with him to our hotels, not suspecting that he would be much more involved in our little story from there on out. Foreshadowing his luck the rest of the trip, his bags were lost and would not arrive until the next day.

The truth is I am getting spoiled in my old age. There were many years during my Saco days where I stayed in small, Indian-run hotels with rarely more than 22 rooms, often with no phone, and always with bugs and a strong smell of curry emanating from the lobby which also doubled as a home for a big family. I would never pay over $20 a night. Ever. However, I was told by Colon that he got me a really nice hotel with a swimming pool, but it turned out to be a Microtel hotel, a small Motel 6-style place along a highway, "which is much quieter than being in town." The great thing about Colon is that he is very frugal and will insure you don't overspend. He and Edison were headed for a hostel, where you share a room full of bunk beds and one shower for under $5 per night. And while the Microtel was very clean and came with free Internet access, it was very isolated and spartan. This choice foreshadowed some other choices that I would regret Colon making for me later.

December through the first of March is summer in Mendoza, and so it's very warm, around 90 to 95 degrees, but there is virtually no humidity, so it is quite pleasant. Mendoza is the capital of wine making in Argentina with over 1,200 wineries. Their primary export market is England, but they are also widely available in the U.S. too. Workers make around $400 per month, and most dress well, and there are little signs of poverty and a very low cost of living. Argentina is a good place to do business, too, with a flat corporate tax rate of 21%.

Saturday evening we had a great steak dinner with a very good bottle of wine for under $10 each. If you like great wine and arguably the best steaks in the world and only want to pay a third of what you would pay anywhere else, then Mendoza is the place to come.

SUNDAY, FEBRUARY 5TH

To buy a park entrance pass, you must first go to the park office in Mendoza and fill out a few forms. Then you take the forms to a grocery store to pay the fee (about $220 per person) and get one of the forms stamped. Then you return to the park office with the stamped form, and they give you a ticket to enter the park. A bit strange but I think it has something to do with not wanting the park office to hold a lot of cash. From there we were off to Penitentes, elevation 6,400', the last place of lodging prior to entering the park, which is about 15 minutes further.

It was a three-hour drive to Penitentes, and it gave us a chance to get to know Andrew better. Andrew was from Brighton, England, was 37, and had never been mountain climbing before. He had not been married but had a girlfriend who he intended to become more serious with when he returned from this trip. He had traveled extensively, and we enjoyed his stories about trips to Nepal, Thailand, and India. He worked for Unilever in the export department, so in addition to what I considered exotic holidays, he had also been nearly everywhere on business too. The one thing I would learn to admire about Andrew was his attitude. He was never stressed about his lack of knowledge of mountaineering or even of his itinerary (his friend, Steve, who was due to join him a couple of days later, had done all the planning). He enjoyed every hour and the experiences around him. He never complained about cold, etc., but instead marveled at the exceptional beauty around him.

We arrived around 2:00 p.m. at a hostel operated by Campo Base, our outfitter. It's a very small place with three rooms downstairs, each the size of a large closet and each with four to five bunk beds in them. We spent an hour or so on the front porch spreading out our gear and reorganizing it. Some things we would carry in our back packs for the next three days, during which time it was supposed to be warmer, putting the rest of the gear we would need for the high camps and our summit bid in duffel bags to be carried by mules to Plaza de Mules, the high camp, and then our city clothes, etc. in another duffel to be left at the hostel.

In the winter, Penitentes is a ski resort with a few small hotels, a couple of very small restaurants, and a gas station. It was the night of the Super Bowl, and there were satellite dishes in the windows of the two nearby restaurants, but when we checked, none had access, and we were just able to watch DVDs.

We hiked up the ski hill for about an hour and gained a 1,000' of elevation to 9,500' and then returned down. Then we went in search of a phone so that I could call home since the hostel didn't have one. We found a phone booth across the street by the gas station, but we had no change. We first tried two small hostels on that side of the highway with no luck. As a last resort, we stopped into the only hotel that was open. To our surprise and my good fortune, they had not only an indoor phone booth, you could pay for the phone call at the desk, and there was a big sitting area with a television with satellite. And the Super Bowl pregame show was on! I bought each of us a beer and began explaining the game to Colon and Edison. After about 30 minutes, they went away to check on something and then came back with a key to a room at the hotel for me. It was still very cheap, about $20 for the night, but it was a great luxury to have a room with my own shower and a functioning toilet.

The Campo Base hostel in Penintentes. The scenery was amazing. The 1959 Uva Russian bus was very exotic looking but did not have reverse or a parking break.

We went back to the hostel for dinner around 8:00. The manager of the hostel, who is the only one there and thus does everything, came in and apologized for dinner saying he had no meat and thus we would be having a vegetarian dish. When it was served, it was a very tasty, lentil stew. However, we noticed small chucks of beef in it. We had a good laugh and decided that in Argentina, a vegetarian dish meant that there was less than a half pound of beef involved.

After dinner, which seemed interminably long, I rushed back to the lodge and to the Super Bowl only to find I had missed only ten minutes worth of the game, such is the pace of Super Bowls. They are not nearly as much fun to watch in Spanish, and the commercials are just the run of the mill spots they would have for any Latin American show. Still, it was a fun being able to reconnect with a little bit of home for a few hours.

MONDAY, FEBRUARY 5TH

We were all up by 7:00 a.m. and had breakfast by 8:00, but we had to wait around until 1:00 to get picked up by the Campo Base bus. It was a short drive to the park entrance, and we were on the trail by 1:30. As we were setting off, a helicopter arrived with a climber they had evacuated. The helicopter made frequent trips carrying supplies in and out to the two "developed" camps above, Confuencia, where we were heading today, and Plaza de Mules or base camp, where one sets off from to climb the mountain.

Confluencia means confluence in English and is so named became it is where two rivers join to make the Mendoza river.

Our relationship with Andrew was a little awkward. I had paid for two guides with lots of experience to accompany me. Andrew, while a nice guy, really didn't have a clue about what he was doing. A friend had talked him into the trip and was supposed to meet him in a couple of days. He had never climbed anything before and was using gear that a friend had lent him that he had never used before. He had no walking sticks, outdated boots, and no plan on how to approach the mountain. He also noted that while he ran a half marathon in December, it was the first real exercise he had done since school (he is now 37, unmarried, living in Brighton, England) and hasn't done much since. He asked if he could tag along with us, and my guides were a little pressed on how to respond. On the approach to base camp, I didn't see any harm in him hanging out with us. We could share with him what we could, but once on the mountain we didn't want to be responsible for him. One always hears of horror stories at any mountain, and we were afraid that Andrew had the makings of one.

Andrew Turton, our unplanned but enjoyable companion.

It took us three hours to get to Confluencia, about a seven- mile hike with an altitude gain of 1,400' to 10,900'. We were walking quite slowly in order to give our bodies an easier time of acclimatization. I also got my first taste of the wind and how quickly the weather changed.

On the way up, we passed about a half-dozen climbers coming down looking very weather beaten with scabs for mouths. Andrew noted that no one was smiling, but I would have imagined their lips would split if they had. In addition to probably what was a very tough day before, I would learn later that it is a 25-mile hike out from Plaza de Mules to the park entrance, and even though it is a loss of 4,000', it is rolling with some sharp inclines mixed in and no matter, just a long, long hike.

It was nonetheless a beautiful hike. We crossed one bridge over a small river that we would follow most of the way up to Plaza de Mules. I was told the bridge was built for Brad Pitt for the movie, *Seven Years in Tibet*. Beforehand, one had to cross the stream, about 20' across with small rapids and about 2' deep. We all thanked Brad Pitt. I haven't seen the movie but will. If you want to get a good idea of the beauty of the landscape, you should watch the movie as it was all filmed here, not in Tibet.

When we got to the camp, I was surprised at how big it was. There were five different outfitters each with about a half-dozen big tents, one for cooking, one dining tent, and then the rest were sleeping tents, each holding about eight people. In addition, there were probably 30 backpacking tents set up, a dozen small porta-potty-style bathrooms (each outfitter had their own and you had to use a key), a park check-in station, and a medical hut.

In my "lucky hat" that Jenny knitted me just before departure.

The medical hut was something I had never seen before, and it was very handy. It was encouraged that everyone go each day and check on their blood pressure, heart rate ,and blood oxygen level. On this day, my blood pressure was 150/90, which is normal for me, and the important oxygen blood level was 92, which is very good. To be healthy at altitude, it needs to be at least over 74. Below that, you are in trouble. Edison seemed very pleased with the 92.

The camp was eclectic though not as much as I would find Plaza de Mules later. Outside our tents was a volleyball court and at around 5:00 p.m. each day, a game would break out primarily amongst the staff from all the outfitters, but others could join in, too. It was funny to see volleyball at 11,000'. Even funnier, with every spike, the ball would go off either bouncing into a tent or several hundred' away. They spent more time chasing after the ball than playing, but they seemed undeterred.

Volleyball at Confluencia, elevation 10,800'.

Staff at both camps were an interesting lot. Most had dreadlocks, rarely bathed, and all were young, maybe in their late 20s. They would arrive for the season in November and stay until the first of March. It was a very Bohemian lifestyle.

That night at dinner, we met a college student from New Zealand just trekking for a couple of days and Raymond, from the Netherlands, attempting Aconcagua for the second time.

I have mixed emotions about dinner at camp. On the one hand, I hate it. There is something about mountains in the late afternoon. It can be pleasant and sunny in the afternoon, but around 5:00 or 6:00, the wind starts picking up and reaches 20 to 30 mph and since it is coming down and around the peaks, it is a very cold wind. The temperature drops from 60 degrees to 20 or 30. The dining tent is of course not heated, and so you put on everything you brought to stay warm. Since I expected it to be warm the first two days, I wasn't well prepared. Either way, dinner is a meal of a light soup and some type of pasta dish, and we all sat around shivering, but there is really no alternative other than wrapping up in the sleeping bag.

However, what I do love is meeting the other people and talking. It is always a very international and interesting group. At this camp, we got to know the young man from New Zealand.

Raymond, who we would see the next four nights, shared his experience of his first climb seven years earlier. It was a disaster. The trip was organized by someone from the Netherlands who apparently had little or no experience with high-altitude climbing. There were 26 of them, but they only brought five stoves with them. Thus, at the two highest camps, they couldn't melt snow fast enough to make water, and so all were very dehydrated. Most didn't bring the proper gear. One of the climbers brought some cheap gloves,and as a result, his hands were badly frostbitten, and he had to have nine fingers removed, keeping only one thumb. Another one in the party didn't bring goggles, only sunglasses, and one of his eyes froze. Of the 26, five summited and all survived, but it was a very unpleasant experience. Raymond was climbing alone this time, but had all the right gear. Raymond was a fun guy to be around. He was always smiling and laughing, and we would see him each night from here on out.

TUESDAY, FEBRUARY 6TH

We woke around 7:30 this morning and had a leisurely breakfast of toast with butter and jam and tea. While cold in the dining tent, it was bearable, and the conversation was good. We set off at 9:20 a.m. for what was to be a four hour hike to Francia camp, an abandoned campsite at the foot of the South Face of Aconcagua. This was an acclimatization hike of roughly seven miles with an elevation gain of 2,000' to 12,900'.

Andrew set off about five minutes before us in short pants even though the wind was blowing and making it a little chilly. When we started, Edison took the lead and walked very slowly, rightly wanting us to focus more on slow acclimatization and less on strength and conditioning. However, a couple of groups passed us, and at the first break about an hour into the trek, I asked to lead and roughly doubled our pace. Frustratingly, while we overtook everyone else, we never caught up with Andrew. We arrived at Francia at 12:00 or in 2 hours and 40 minutes.

The very difficult, yet beautiful South Face.

We took a long lunch at Francia while taking in the awe inspiring South Face. Edison and Colon could point out the routes that other climbers took including Rheinhold Messner, one of the most famous and accomplished climbers alive today. On his first attempt, he summited in 14 hours but his partner broke his leg about four hours from the summit. Messner went back down, got his partner, and carried him to the top. The photo of the South Face doesn't do its difficulty justice – it really does look impossible, and for Messner to do a summit in that short of a time seems incredible, but to go down, pick someone up, and carry them back up is truly superhuman.

A close friend of Colon's tried to match Messner's time a couple of years ago. He only packed enough for a day. However, he got bad weather two-thirds of the way up the South Face and had to stay put for another 24 hours. Late on his second day, he was dangerously out of water, food, and very cold. The base station radioed him telling him to come down, but he couldn't hear them and kept going to the summit, which he made on his third day. To get down, he went from the slightly lower South summit over to the North summit, from which it is easier to descend. However, he was so exhausted that he passed out and slept for 24 hours there. Another group of climbers came up the North route, saw his body, and assumed he was dead and headed down. When he awoke after 24 hours, he managed to descend; however, his feet were badly frostbitten, and he had to have all 10 toes and half his left foot removed.

We hurried back taking 1 hour and 50 minutes on the return and were back in camp by 2:30. After a few hours passed, we began to worry about Andrew, but he finally showed up at 5:30, having gone just a bit further than we did and lingering longer taking in the view. He didn't wear a watch, so he wasn't sure how long he spent there or on the return.

On our return, there was nothing to do at camp, so I got into my sleeping bag and read for four hours. I think I chose the wrong book for many reasons. I chose *Lincoln: A Team of Rivals*, which is a hardback of 800 pages and weighs a ton. Further, every page involves a father, mother, wife, or child dying in someone's family at a very young age. It focused on how all these politicians were separated from their families and how much they all missed each other. This is not the proper material to read when you are away from home.

On the medical check that night, my blood pressure remained the same, but my blood oxygen content had risen to 96%, which is very good. I was acclimatizing well this trip. We had dinner at around 8:30 that night, which consisted of some very good spaghetti. To escape the cold, we all went to our sleeping bags at 9:00 p.m. and didn't rise until 8:00 a.m. the next morning.

WEDNESDAY, FEBRUARY 7TH

After our breakfast of toast with butter, jam, and tea and saying good bye to the New Zealand student and our cook, we set off for Plaza de Mules. The hike is through the Horcones Valley, 18 miles gaining 3,000' of elevation and along a fast-moving river that is the color of mud. It is deep, wide, and full of rapids at the start but then gets clear and narrow further up. While I took many photos, they simply don't do the area justice. Unfortunately, the 10-20 mph wind was in my face most of the way up, often pelting me with dust, and the trail is very rocky, so you have your head down most of the way. However, when I did take a moment to look around, it was incredible. The jagged mountains on each side were luminescent shades of green rock in very angular, sharp formations. In spots, there was some green vegetation in the valley, but it was mostly rock as you would expect from a dried-up river bed, which it all was at one time. I would highly recommend someone just coming on the trip for a hike through the Horcones Valley. It would be worth the trip.

Colon said the hike would be long and hard and take us eight to nine hours, but we actually did it in seven hours. There were a few fairly steep segments, but it was mostly a flat-to-gentle incline. And while most sections were in a river bed, there were several sections along cliffs 200' or so above the river. While providing some dramatic vistas, these passages also added a small bit of excitement too.

About once an hour, we would have to step away from the trail for mule caravans that were portaging supplies either to or from Plaza de Mules. They are amazing animals that I never really appreciated until now. They could carry two 50-kilo packs and go very fast up and down these treacherous, narrow, rock-strewn trails. We discussed the option of riding them back at the end of the trip. One could be hired for about $140 for the one-way trip, but after some discussion, we decided it would be too scary and decided we would rather take our chances on our
own feet.

We arrived at Plaza de Mulas, elevation 13,684', around 4:00 p.m., which I'll describe in more detail later. We had our climbing gear and food sent up via mule, and reconnecting with all of this was like Christmas. There were our warmer coats, pants, gloves, etc. which we wished we had packed earlier. Unfortunately, Colon had packed some honey in one of the bags which busted, so there was honey on his down coat, on my duffel bag, and a few other places. Removing honey from our gear was our project for the evening.

Arriving at Plaza de Mules, 13,684', which is in a valley surrounded by 20,000' plus mountains.

At dinner that night we met Martin, a 45-year-old Australian who had done some climbing in the Andes. He was an interesting guy who really didn't look like a climber nor did he seem very prepared nor did he seem very concerned about any discomfort or risk. He was married to a Peruvian girl and lived with her in Australia, where he worked for an environmental agency. He was on a six-month vacation by himself through South America, staying with friends and in hostels. He also became a concern of ours. He didn't bring much food for his summit attempt so was always very happy to get any donation. His tent was basically a sheet wrapped around poles, possibly appropriate for the back yard on a clear summer day. And he had this strange idea that if he didn't wear his gloves in base camp that his hands would somehow become better able to deal with the cold later on. We all liked Martin, but he was a concern and like Andrew, seemed like a living example of how people get hurt on mountains.

Fine dining at Plaza de Mules.

Also, we met Alejandro from Spain, but he did not speak English well, so I didn't get to know him. Dinner conversations would alternate between all English with Alejandro being left out, all Spanish with Andrew and I straining to pick out enough words to follow along, or two separate conversations in each language. Topics ranged from the politics of each one's country to mountain climbing to life ambitions (never economic ones, though) to families or dreams of having one. I was the only one married with children, but the others, in particular Edison and Colon, were very disappointed about not having a family of their own.

We also discussed Aconcagua and our strategies for climbing it. Someone commented that over the last three days, no one had summitted and that one climber had come down from Camp Berlin complaining of chest-high snow in one section. It is always windy and cold, but the last couple of weeks had been particularly so.

We turned in around 9:00 p.m., and while I would usually read for a while by headlamp, it had been such a long day that I went right to bed. By the way, sleeping at altitude is not easy. One usually has many very vivid dreams and wakes regularly. Also, the correct thing to do is to continue to hydrate (drinks lots of fluids) right up to bedtime and even when you wake during the night, as you do often. However, I purposely did not on this trip to avoid the hike to the toilet. With so many people at camp, to keep it sanitary, it is necessary to use the portable toilets. Each camp outfitter had their own that was locked up. So to go, you first had to find your headlamp, get on your fleece pants, shoes (I brought Crocs just for this purpose so I could put them on and off quickly), hat and heavy coat, then go get the key, then walk about 200' up and down a couple of small hills and around some tents to use the toilet. It is a real pain and makes you appreciate the small luxuries of home like being able to simply get out of bed in a warm house to go to the bathroom.

THURSDAY, FEBRUARY 8TH

Thursday was a scheduled rest day. When at altitude, one's body works very hard to adapt to the lower oxygen content in the air, and it's important to allow it time to do this with minimum activity. However, for me, it allowed too much time to think and reflect. We rose and had breakfast a little later. Everyone else at Campo Base was also taking a rest day, so we lingered at breakfast for some time. There was also a "recreation tent" with a chess board and some more comfortable chairs to sit in and read, and we would congregate there.

I did explore the camp, which was a very surreal place. Colon had told me it was like a small city with over "2000 people," but he apparently got his words confused as there were only about 200 people, about one-third of which were staff. There were at least four tents that offered Internet and satellite service, two tents that offered themselves as restaurants serving pizza and burgers, a tent that offered hot showers (they couldn't get them to work the day I was there), and strangely, an artist with the "world's highest art gallery" which was in a large, walk-in tent (he was also right next to the shower tent, but judging from his smell, he had not found his way there since the season began in November, or it had not worked for a very long, long time).

The "art gallery" with some whimsical direction signs out front.

Geotrek sold hamburgers, pizza, beer, and Internet. We didn't try it, but I was told by Raymond, who did, that you had to keep in mind the conditions they were cooking in to appreciate them.

Colon had told me there was a lodge a kilometer away that some people would mule or helicopter to just for sightseeing and doing some light trekking in the area, so we decided to hike over to it for something to do. I asked if they might have showers for hire, and he said they might, so I took my toilet kit with me. When we got there, I was surprised at how big it was. It was three stories, and though rustic, had a game room with a ping-pong table, a semi-open bar area with a fireplace, and most importantly, a place to take a hot shower and a lounge area and dining hall that was heated. For U.S. $10, I got to take a seven minute shower. It was wonderful! Afterwards, we had a Pepsi in the lobby area that had a great view of Aconcagua and our route. Also, I noticed a huge stack of climbing gear duffels either having just arrived or ready to head down. As I'll note later, there are other more comfortable ways to approach this climb, which include using this lodge, and that if I return in the future, will be part of the plan the next time.

On the hike back to our camp, the sun had come out, and it was around 50 degrees Fahrenheit with not much wind. I really did feel great. Two hours later we had sleet, snow, rain, and temperatures in the 20s, and the wind was back up to 10 to 20 mph gusts.

Before dinner, I went to the medical tent and my heart rate was the same, but my blood oxygen was down to 82. Edison said this is normal. Below 74 would be insufficient to climb though toward the summit, it would likely drop to well below 60, which is why you don't want to linger at those altitudes.

Around 5:00 p.m., a message was delivered to Andrew by one of the Campo Base staff. It was from his long-awaited friend Steve, but was unfortunately bad news. Steve said he had arrived at Confluencia but was suffering from the altitude. He was vomiting and had severe headaches and had decided to go back down and return to Dubai. They had planned this 15-day climb together followed by several days in Rio de Janeiro for Carnival, and it was now being aborted by his friend after just a couple of days. I was really impressed with Andrew, however, who was unflappable. He was neither despondent nor bitter.

There were some spectacular views from camp like this one near sunset on Thursday night.

Colon, Edison, and I stepped outside the tent and discussed Andrew. My guides were concerned that they had not been hired by Andrew and did not want to get distracted by him and further, they were not sure he would make it. Edison said he was selective about who he guided, and he would have refused to take on Andrew due to his conditioning, inexperience, and inappropriate gear. But we all liked Andrew, and they left it to me to decide. I recommended that we let him follow along with us to Nido de Condores or Camp Berlin, and then on summit day he could follow, but if he decided to turn back, he would be on his own. We went back into the tent and informed him of this, and he was very happy.

However, I did this with much consternation. For the last three days, I had alternated nearly hourly from confidence and eagerness to take on the challenges ahead to utter misery and futility. Lying in a sleeping bag for 12 hours a day gives one way too much time to think. Listening to the stories of frostbitten fingers and toes being removed, of waist-deep snow preventing summiting, and of exceptionally high winds began to weigh on me and my calculations of the probability of making it. Also, the continuous cold, the stench, the heroic but less than appetizing food, the toilets, and the constant battle with altitude was fatiguing. Per our schedule, the most optimistic plan would mean another eight days on the mountain, but likely another ten.

That evening before dinner we checked with the weather forecast at one of the tents with Internet. Friday was suppose to be clear and nice, but that evening a storm was due in that would last for two to three days. After which, it was hoped to be clear again. Edison, Colon, and I sat in the tent and discussed a revised plan. On Friday, we would climb all the way to Nido de Condores, store some gear, and then come back down. Saturday, we would take another acclimatization hike either to Camp Canada or all the way back to Nido again, even in a storm. Sunday we would take a rest day in Plaza de Mules, and then Monday, hopefully with clear weather, go back to Nido where we would spend the night. If we felt strong the next morning, we could go for the summit. Alternatively, we could take another rest day there and go to the summit the following day. Or we could stick to the original plan which was then to carry gear up to Berlin, go back and spend the night in Nido, then the following day climb up to Berlin, spend the night there, and then summit; the following day.

From Nido it is ten hours to the summit from Berlin it is eight. Most go from Berlin, but the camp is extraordinarily windy, and it is very hard to sleep there.

Planning the details of the climb was always good to create a positive frame of mind. However, sitting at dinner with Colon, Edison, and the rest, I determined I had had enough. After dinner I informed Colon and Edison of my decision. I had a great trip, met some interesting people, and had experiences I would remember all my life, but I was just too miserable. The idea of freezing for another eight days or so, a few of which would be in much, much worse conditions, and with a very low probability of success along with higher than normal possibility of loss of life or body parts, I just didn't want to continue. I was surprised at how supportive they were. They confessed that they were miserable too, and that they understood but did suggest that I sleep on it and decide in the morning.

FRIDAY, FEBRUARY 9TH

I didn't sleep much the night before, waking at 3:00 a.m. and laying in the sleeping bag until 6:45. I spent the first few hours debating my decision, but when I finally concluded it was time to head back down, then I spent the rest of the time calculating every detail from how I would pack to what I would do on both my return to Mendoza and then to Knoxville.

I got up at around 6:45 a.m. and went to the bathroom and when I returned, I noticed Edison was awake. I confirmed my decision, and he and Colon both rose, and we all started preparing for our descent. I woke Andrew and told him, "I hate that you are getting stood up twice in 12 hours, but I am heading back." Again, he seemed calm and unperturbed. Colon and Edison assured him that he could probably tag along with another group, and we subsequently got acknowledgment of that from Martin and Raymond. He wasn't sure of a summit this trip, but with every step up, he was setting a new personal record, and he just wanted to see how far he could go. His next goal was Nido de Condores, and then he would decide from there. I think his is the right approach. One should take it literally one step at a time. If you think of the whole process, it can become overwhelming, which is what I allowed myself to do.

*The view of Aconcagua from Base Camp. We were in a "valley"
at nearly 14,000'.*

I considered just sneaking out, but I am glad I didn't, though it would
have been impossible. As my camp mates heard I was leaving, they all came
out to say goodbye. First, Edison wanted a photo of us with Andrew which
started a series of group photos, and soon we had everyone in the camp in
the picture. Trying to leave was like being the first to leave at a family
reunion. It is amazing how close you can come to others in such a short
period of time when under unusual or challenging circumstances. Verbally,
I wished them all good luck, but internally, I wished for them to just be
prudent and return safely.

Departing. From left to right; Edison, Colon, Martin, Alejandro, Raymond, Andrew, and Randy.

The hike out was uneventful but fast. We left at 9:20 a.m. and managed to complete what was normally a ten hour hike in six hours, arriving back at the park entrance by 3:30 including a 45 minute lunch break back at Confluencia. Of course, it helped that we were very fresh and were not tired from a summit bid a day or two before as would be the case for most. Still, it was a two-mile hike at altitude. I can only imagine how grueling it would have seemed to do after eight more days and a summit bid.

We arrived back in Mendoza by 7:00 p.m. that night, in time for me to arrange new flights to depart on Sunday and to call home and let Jenny know of my new plans. She was supportive and looking forward to having me back. After a long, hot shower, a shave, and slipping on some clean clothes, I walked to one of the outdoor cafés on a very pretty pedestrian street and ordered pizza and wine. I was warm and euphoric, but my mind was still split – half of me was back with my family and looking forward to doing those things that normally might seem mundane but experiences like these make you appreciate; the other half was still on the mountain with Martin, Andrew, Raymond, and Alejandro feeling their cold, their ambition, and hoping for their success but mostly for their safety.

EPILOGUE

I am happy about this trip. Someone emailed me when I announced I was returning that "We're glad to have you back, but I know how much you hate to fail." In one sense, this is true. However, as Edison and Colon and I discussed at length, mountaineering is about much more than summiting. You are only on the top for one minute or so, and while it does fill you with a great sense of accomplishment, it is really about the entire experience. And while this experience was cut short, it was still a good one.

I had two takeaways as a result of this trip. First, I reconfirmed to myself that while I enjoy summit day, the long, arduous challenge of ten or more hours of climbing, of testing one's will and endurance; I don't care for long expeditions where the approach and acclimatization process takes weeks. Thus, unless I change my attitude on such things, I won't be climbing the six or seven summits since all but one of these requires such an expedition.

However, I have not given up on Aconcagua though I will approach it differently the next time. On my return, I will repeat the first three days of this trip but instead stay at the lodge rather than Plaza de Mules. I think warm showers each day, dining in my t-shirt, and a comfortable place to read and relax will help my attitude. I will also allow three weeks. Each day I will set off for Nido de Condores or maybe even Berlin, building my stamina and acclimatization. Meanwhile, I can patiently, but comfortably, wait for good weather. Then I can take the summit with a two-day approach having my gear already at Nido or Berlin. I can hike there early the first morning, rest until midmorning the next day (3:00 a.m.), and then head up. I doubt this will be in the next four or five years (I would like to see Harrison off to college first), but I look forward to trying it. Even if I don't summit, I want to see how far up the mountain I can go. I'll be happy with the experience.

Second, I fell in love with Mendoza, and Jenny and I decided to buy a small vineyard. The city is beautiful, with tree-lined streets, friendly people, and the best steaks in the world at the cities' best restaurants for around $7. There are over 1,200 wineries to tour within 100 miles, the climate is great, and the Andes are always within sight, just two hours away. Jenny and I will be spending a winery touring holiday there next year. If not for this trip, none of this would have happened. Destiny can be unpredictable.

Thus, this is a strange and atypical narrative from my previous three. Most importantly, it misses the march to the top. Even as I write these final words, I don't know if it is worth reading; however, I did want to write it. The memories are so strong and rich that I hate to lose them, and hopefully, one cold day by a warm fire in my old age, I can reread these notes, and it can bring back to life what was a great experience. For those reading, I hope you consider trekking the Horcones Valley one day or at least driving to the park to see Aconcagua for a break during your tours of the wineries in Mendoza. At the very least, please order a bottle of Mendoza wine the next time you are out to dinner – maybe it might be a wine from our vineyard!

POSTSCRIPT

I got an email from Andrew on February 18th. He contracted bronchitis the day we left and was sick for four days. However, he recovered and was able to climb to Berlin at 5,930 meters before he left, which is his new personal record.

Additional Postscript May 30th, 2007

-----Original Message-----

From: "info" <info@peak-adventure-travel.com>
To: "'Randy Boyd'" <rboyd@petsafe.net>

Sent: 5/30/07 8:26 PM

Subject: Bad news

Hi Randy,

This is Edison. I haven't been in touch for many reasons but now I'm writing you just to inform that a terrible accident happened one week ago. Colon had a terrible climbing accident and unfortunately he passed away. It's been hard for me and many other friends.

Deeply Sad,
Edison

-----Mensaje original-----

De: Randy Boyd [mailto:rboyd@petsafe.net]
Enviado el: Wednesday, May 30, 2007 8:08 PM Para: info

Asunto: RE: Bad news

Dear Edison,

This is very tragic news. I don't know what to say, but my prayers and sympathies are with you and his family. When you are up to it, I would like to know what happened. He was so skilled & had such a practical attitude. I'm just shocked now,
but if there is anything I can do just let me know.

Your Friend,
Randy

Following on May 31st after requesting more detail.

Dear Randy,

The past week it's been really hard but everything is getting back to normal. Well, Colon took two cousins and two uncles to Rucu Pichincha; they were inexperienced and they went over the ridge on a place named "Paso de la muerte." He placed a rope for protection and made the people cross it safely, when he returned to recover his rope it started to rain and obviously the rock got slippery and according to one of his cousins they saw Colon falling and within a second he disappeared, since that moment they were screaming to him but no response.

Around 4 p.m. I got a phone call from a friend saying that Colon is lost somewhere in Rucu Pichincha and right away I started calling to some people from the ASEGUIM (the Mountain Guides Association) to get started with a rescue patrol. The bottom line is that they found him around 2 am.

Is hard to write this but as a friend and mountaineer I think is important try to briefly explain the facts. Thanks for offering your help and if something will be needed I'll let you know. Likewise, if there's something that I can do don't hesitate to ask.

Stay in Touch,
Ed

Rucu Pichincha – Rest in peace my friend.

CHAPTER 18

BOSTON MARATHON 2013

The quest of every marathoner is to qualify for the Boston Marathon, and depending on one's gender and age, the qualifying time is different. However, even if you qualify, you still have to enter a lottery and hope to be selected. On the other hand, by raising a certain amount for a charity, you can run with their team. Knowing that and not sure if I would qualify, in the fall of 2011 I joined the uAspire Team, which is a college advising non-profit, very appropriate for me. My best time that year was at the New York City Marathon in which I finished at 3 hours and 38 minutes. Sadly, my qualifying time was insufficient. I would be able to run in Boston but not as an official qualifier.

Boston is called the grandfather of marathons, being one of the oldest in the country. Besides its history, it was one of the most fun races to run due to all the great support from the fans. It's run on a Monday, and the city celebrates a "Patriots Day" holiday, so all businesses are closed, allowing for more Bostonians to come out and cheer on the runners, and they do. Running by Wellesley, an all-girls college, the coeds stand alongside the road with funny signs saying, "Kiss me, I'm a Physics Major" or "Kiss me, I'm from Argentina," etc. The Boston Red Sox have a game that starts at 10:00 a.m., so the fans let out about the time that the bulk of the runners pass by the stadium. All along the 26.2-mile course, fans are cheering. The finish is down the famous but quaint shopping street, Boyleston, that temporarily houses stands for the fans. All along the course, there is tremendous support from enthusiastic Bostonians. Jenny loves Boston and enjoys accompanying me.

The 2012 marathon was one of the hottest on record, starting the race in the 80s and finishing in the 90s. It was so hot that the night before, organizers were offering runners the opportunity to take a deferred entry for the following year. If you ran, they advised to take it slow. I did run, but it was my slowest in nearly ten years. I finished, looking forward to redemption the following year.

I ran three more marathons in 2012 but again did not qualify, so I decided to run with uAspire once more in April, 2013. While a bit cooler, it was still warm enough to cause dehydration, and I started cramping toward the end. I ran through the finish scanning the stands for Jenny who was supposed to be there to cheer me on, but I didn't see her. This happens often as there are so many runners and so many fans that it's easy to miss each other.

I walked the first block from the finish line, where runners receive their medal and a water bottle. My muscles were cramping a lot, and I was worried they would go into spasms, which has happened to me a few times and is a very scary feeling, so I decided to stand next to the First Aid station just in case. After ten minutes since crossing the finish line two blocks behind me, I heard the sound of a loud cannon. My first reaction was puzzlement. Why would they be firing a canon in the middle of the race? I turned around toward the finish line and saw debris and smoke shooting from the building to the right of the finish line. In that instant, a second blast occurred, and I immediately realized we were under some sort of attack.

In the same instant, I thought of Jenny. She was supposed to be in the stands at the finish line right where the blasts occurred. Surely she saw me pass and has already left and was on her way back to the hotel where we were to meet.

I continued to tell myself that over and over as I, like all the runners, began moving steadily from the direction of the blasts as organizers were encouraging us to do. At that moment no one knew what was happening. Was it bombs, were they being fired from some other location, and were there more on the way? All were tired but moved hurriedly in surprisingly organized fashion away from the scene and toward the baggage claim area another several blocks away.

I couldn't wait to get to my gear bag I had checked before the race because it had my phone in it, and I could call Jenny to see that she was ok. When I finally retrieved and turned on my phone, I discovered that security had jammed all cellular service. It turns out this is standard practice in such emergencies because many bombs are activated by phones. But it gave me no way to find Jenny and to see if she was ok.

Now my conversation with myself changed to convincing myself Jenny would be in the hotel waiting for me. I made my way to the hotel, another five blocks away, as fast as I could. Arriving at the hotel, I went up the elevator and into the room, only to find the room empty. My heart sank, and all my rationalizations began to melt away. Panic began to set in. I tried the hotel phone to call her, but she didn't answer. I turned on the TV to find out what was happening and began to learn the details of the attack and the carnage at the finish. More panic. I tried Jenny's phone again. No answer.

Then she walked in the room. Our embrace was intense, and as one should never have to be reminded but sometimes needs to be, nothing is more cherished than those you love. We were the lucky ones. Some didn't have family members come back to them, and some came back permanently disabled. God had other plans for us on that day, and we are thankful. The moral of the story is an obvious one – cherish those you love and keep them close.

THE STORY FROM JENNY'S PERSPECTIVE

The year prior to the bombing, I had a special pass to sit in the stands to watch Randy finish the race. This particular year, I also had that same privilege, but a funny thing happened. I was a block away from the stands getting ready to cross the street when I noticed how great the sun felt on my face and thought it would be a warm place to wait for Randy. Not long after is when the first bomb went off. I thought it was fireworks or a cannon, but that didn't add up. Then the second blast came. The police immediately started taking down the barricades that lined the street, and people started screaming. It was very surreal. I think for the next 30 minutes, I just stood there and scanned the crowd for Randy. The buses were lined up waiting for the runners, so I thought I would run into him there. I still wasn't sure what had transpired. I tried calling Randy, our kids, anyone really, and none of my calls were getting through. Now it had been about 40 minutes since the blasts. I now could hear a man yelling "Jenny, Jenny" apparently trying to locate a loved one. I took this as a sign to get moving as it made me realize that I had been standing there quite a while. I headed back down the street to our hotel, which was at the end of this very busy road, and as I got closer, I saw that people really didn't have a clue as to what had just happened at the marathon. People were shopping, having lunch, talking with friends, etc. I wanted to just shout at them that I didn't know where my husband was and that there was a bombing. There were police stationed at the door of our hotel, and we had to show proof that we were guests before they would let me in. I was in tears and disbelief. I didn't know what I would do if Randy hadn't made it back to the room. Who would I call to find that out? As I opened the door to the hotel room, I felt tremendous relief, and I couldn't believe he made it back before me. I believe in divine guidance, and I know that we were in God's hands that day.

CHAPTER 19

HUGO'S VISION
November 6, 2016

Hugo has a vision. He dreams of running. Fast. He dreams of running fast enough to make the Peruvian National Team. He dreams of going to a university and getting a degree. If he can make the national team, then he can get a scholarship to go to college. That is his vision. That is his dream.

Hugo Estrada was born in the Peruvian jungle 31 years ago on a farm where his father grows cocoa and coffee. Growing up with his eight siblings, he enjoyed walking and running back from school. But it was not an idyllic, rural setting. It was a time when the Shining Path, communist revolutionaries, terrorized the countryside. At age 12, Hugo developed Retinitis Pigmentosa and began to gradually go blind.

Peruvian culture isn't kind to the blind. Often children are put in boarding schools for blind children, but they aren't free. Parents often drop them off, pay for two months boarding in advance, and never come back for them. The school then turns them out in the street. Hugo stayed with his family, but they were not very supportive. He left the jungle for Lima, the capitol, three years ago and was incredibly fortunate to meet Claudia, his girlfriend, and together they are making a life in their one-room apartment (bathrooms are communal). Determined to get the education that was interrupted in the jungle, he hopes to earn the equivalent of a high-school diploma next year. He has already earned a certificate in therapy and works at a spa. In his spare time, he makes crafts for extra money. Between grants and gifts, he was able to make the trip to New York, his first time on a plane and first time out of Peru.

I've run 31 marathons prior to this year, and this made nine New York

City marathons in a row. Every year I would either pass or be passed by Team Achilles, an organization that guides Athletes With Disabilities (AWD). Although I run for Team for Kids, an organization that provides shoes to inner city kids in New York, it's really more a donation, and I never have any direct interaction with the kids. I signed up to run with Achilles too this year, but was first told there was no need for an additional guide, and then there was a cancellation. I got matched with Hugo.

Vincent Lau, an ophthalmologist of Vietnamese decent living in Los Angeles has guided in six other races, and the two of us were paired with Hugo. Claudia emailed us beforehand that his target was 3:55, which is a very serious goal for a first marathon. We met Saturday before the race and learned that while he did his first half marathon in August, his longest training run was only 18 miles. This was disconcerting, and Vincent and I developed a strategy with him with Claudia as our translator. In spite of his goal, we assured him the most important objective on his first marathon was to finish and have fun, but we would try to put him in a position to achieve his goal. We would start out running 8:30 miles for the first 13 miles, making sure we had strength to have a strong second half. Hugo agreed.

On race day Hugo was quiet but confident. He speaks no English and Vincent and I very little Spanish, but enough to guide. There are usually three guides, with two out front to clear a path through the 55,000 runners and one tethered to the runner. Vincent agreed to be the one to tether to Hugo, Vincent's right arm to Hugo's left. I was the "rabbit" in charge of leading by about five meters, setting the pace, clearing traffic, and fetching water for them at the water stations.

One of the fun parts about the New York City Marathon is that it is so international, with on average 130 countries represented. In years past I recall guides yelling "make way, blind runner coming through," and we'd all move to the right or left to let them pass. That part of guiding shouldn't be too much of a problem I didn't presume. Within the first quarter mile, I realized the downside to having such an international field – two out of three runners didn't speak English! For the next 26 miles, I would yell, push, point, and whatever I could think of to clear a path for the two runners trailing me running side by side.

It was also a new experience trying to set a pace for someone else. Rather than running at a pace I felt was right for me, I had a set pace, one a bit slower than I was used to, that I had to meet. During the entire race, my head would be looking to my watch, then behind me to see Vincent and Hugo to make sure they were ok and no one was cutting in front of them, then back ahead. Water stations are very crowded, and people bump into each other a lot so it's not a safe place for the blind runners to go. So my other job was to fall back, get their orders, sprint ahead and grab either water or Gatorade depending on their order, take it to them, sprint back to get some for me, and then run ahead of them again.

By mile 18 we had reached Hugo's furthest he had ever run, and so both Vincent and I began to monitor him more closely. "Come esta?" to which he would always reply, "Bueno," but we would study his stride, his breathing, his arms to make sure he was really ok. Though he began to walk the water stations by mile 26, he remained strong.

It was hard work and thoughtfully tactical, but far, far more rewarding running and winning for someone else. And we did! Hugo was awesome! By mile 24 we knew were going to make it, and by mile 25 we knew we would make his goal. I think I had a big smile on my face the entire last mile to the finish line. Hugo never stopped and finished strong, beating his goal by 32 seconds: 3:54:28!

Hugo inspired Vincent and me with his determination and passion. It is so easy to make excuses, and Hugo could use living in poverty, his blindness, or so many limitations, but he was determined to overcome every obstacle. What excuse could we ever have for anything we would want to accomplish? He also taught us that vision is an ideal, not a physical attribute. Begin with a dream, then create a vision by developing very concrete metrics to measure your progress, like running your first marathon in 3:55. Dream it, envision it, do it. No excuses. Thank you, Hugo. May you continue to achieve your dreams and to inspire others.

A FATHER'S SON

CHAPTER 20

RUNNING WITH THE BULLS

I have strongly encouraged our employees to be active in their work and personal lives. We would frequently conduct employee "bonding" events to build enthusiasm, promote teamwork, and motivate personal development. The story about one of these activities is told by Willie Wallace, our president. It retells an adventure that was beyond "bonding."

Randy and I had participated in a number of runs together starting with the Marine Corp Marathon in Washington D.C. in 2004. Each year we actively ran the half marathon in Knoxville and would find other runs of interest. During one such run, we found ourselves in Southern Utah in October 2007 touring Zion National Park following running the St. George marathon. On the way to the Park in the car, a comment was made on the radio referring to the "Running of the Bulls" during the San Fermin festival in Pamplona, Spain. We both heard it and Randy stated, "I've always wanted to run with the bulls." I retorted that it was on my bucket list as well. Nothing more was spoken about it.

Later in the week, after we had gotten back into the groove of work, I received an email from Randy reading, "Here is our itinerary to run with the bulls in July." I honestly thought it was a joke. The conversation we had in the car certainly didn't come across to me as a commitment to do it or frankly to even consider planning it. But by then, I certainly knew Randy was action-oriented, and after a few moments of thought, I really wasn't surprised. In looking closer at the itinerary, I realized we were indeed going to do this over a long weekend. I don't think I had ever flown to Europe for just a couple of days for either business or work, but that was going to be the case! I hooked up with the travel agent, and we were set to go.

We took off on a Thursday afternoon, and following a long layover in Barcelona, made it to Pamplona, Spain on a small, regional prop plane. A bit sleep deprived, we checked in to our hotel, got a quick nap, and set out to buy the traditional running garb, complete with our new trendy sashes!

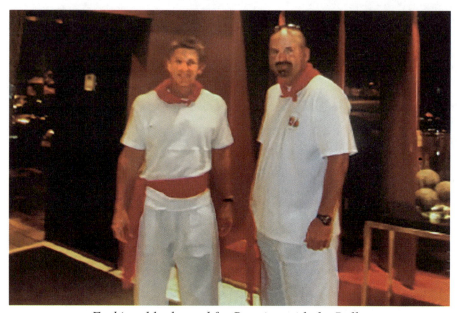

Fashionably dressed for Running with the Bulls.

As the day progressed to evening, we decided to walk down to check out the course and grab some dinner. The "street" in which we were going to try to evade the bulls was little more than an alley and made the New Orleans' famed Bourbon Street look like a sparsely-populated, high-school party. Bars and restaurants on both sides of the streets were packed, and the street was shoulder to shoulder with some very happy festival participants. We grabbed some tapas and got out of there around 10:30 before it got really wild.

We had studied the course of the run in the pamphlets and had decided to get to a spot early before the event started that we thought would be good. We popped out of bed and arrived at the course around 6:15. To our amazement, the party we left at 10:30 the evening before was raging twice as strong at 6:30! At around 7:00, sirens went off, and everyone cleared the street. Street cleaners then came in and picked up all of the broken bottles, cups, and beer cans. Meanwhile, all of the folks who had been partying all night long waited patiently outside of the fence. At ten minutes to 8:00, another whistle blew, and everyone (that is thousands of drunken partiers and two sober Tennesseans!) made our way onto the course. As 8:00 approached, our adrenalin was peaking, and our heart rates were off the chart. We heard the sirens once again that notified the participants that the bulls had been released. It was game time, and the road was so packed I wasn't sure how the bulls were going to get through without mowing down a big swath of people. Randy was just ahead of me and a little to my right when the crowd started shuffling and pushing a little. It finally thinned a little as we picked up steam.

The tricky part of the run is you are looking over your left shoulder as you are running and are not watching what is in front of you, which in this case was a bunch of staggering drunks. As I saw the bulls rumbling toward me, I felt solid contact with somebody and could tell I had knocked them down and to the right. I wasn't about to take my eyes off the bulls and just hoped I hadn't knocked Randy over. The stampede was over as quickly as it had started but seemed to have lasted 30 minutes. It felt like we had run with them a half a mile before we peeled off safely in a doorway and let them pass, but it was probably closer to 75 yards. Randy and I found each other, and as we were catching our breath, putting our hearts back into our chest, and nervously laughing about the experience, out of nowhere here came six more huge animals right at us with huge horns! I thought I was going to soil myself as I heard someone explain they were harmless steers that they send down the street following the bulls to distract a bull that might be working over an unfortunate runner.

Following the run we went to the City Square for a little lunch and Sangria. Over a couple glasses, Randy mentioned that our tour package included a day of running and a day of watching the run from an overhanging balcony. After a couple of glasses of wine for courage, I argued that we would have more fun and be able to run further with them since we knew how it worked, hence, we should run again. I also argued that we hadn't come all the way to "watch the bulls!" What we did, I cannot reveal…what happens in Pamplona stays in Pamplona.

Randy relaxing after Running with the Bulls!

At our next Radio Systems board meeting, we got an earful from our directors about putting ourselves in such a dangerous position together. The fact of the matter is you certainly have more opportunity getting hurt driving to work over a few years than running with those silly bulls. It was however a crazy adrenaline rush and a lot of fun.

EPILOGUE FROM TOM BOYD

While writing this book, I have had the opportunity to review my son's life in business and was surprised at how similar our business experiences have been. The main exception is that he has been quite a bit more successful than I have.

It gave me the opportunity to retrace my steps from the cotton fields of Tennessee through a lifetime of business successes and failures, and, of course, to reflect on my life as a father and the joys of watching my son, Randy, as he followed his path into the world of entrepreneurship and business building.

I hope I have accomplished my goal, which was to pass along the lessons that both Randy and I have learned. I hope the book will provide guidance, inspiration, and encouragement to anyone who wants to start a business.

I stepped outside the business world and added Randy's adventures. These, I hope, will be inspirational in their own right.

I leave you with what I consider to be the four most important guidelines for any entrepreneur:

To quote Winston Churchill, "Never, never, never give up.

Surround yourself with great people.

Always do the right thing.

Be prepared to work harder than you ever thought you could."

TOM BOYD

ABOUT THE AUTHOR
TOM BOYD

The author, Tom Boyd, is a serial entrepreneur who rose from the deep South's cotton fields to become a highly-successful inventor and innovator of problem-solving products. He created Fi-Shock, one of the first electric fences for dogs and livestock; Mark Electronics, a major electronics supplier; I-Shop,Inc., the first online-touchscreen product-purchasing kiosks, which eventually failed due to the introduction of the Internet. This business developed the original format for online purchasing that is available today on Amazon; EDP Biotech, which has developed a test for the early detection of colon cancer; and, BioPet Laboratories, which develops DNA-based animal products. Now an octogenarian, Tom is still active in his business ventures, and continues to foster and champion entrepreneurship. He and his wife, Sandi, make their home in Knoxville, Tennessee.

If you would like to order additional books, either in quantity or individually, please contact the publisher, visit Amazon, or visit BuyTomBoydBooks.com

For speaking engagements or interviews, contact Debbie Patrick, debbie@debbiepatrick.com